CompTIA Security+

Last Minute Revision

400+ acronyms, high-impact examples, and rapid drills mapped to SY0-701 domains for last-minute study

Xandar Pelin

Published by: GitforGits

Publisher: Sonal Dhandre

www.gitforgits.com

Printed in India

First Printing: October 2025

ISBN: 978-93-49174-97-9

Cover Design by: Kitten Publishing

Disclaimer:

This book, including all its text, diagrams, and illustrations, is an original work developed for educational and informational purposes. The content is not affiliated with, endorsed by, or sponsored by CompTIA, or any other company, brand, or entity referenced within. All brand names, product names, and trademarks mentioned are the property of their respective owners and are used in a descriptive, educational context only. Every effort has been made to ensure that no copyrighted or trademarked material has been copied or misused in this book. All diagrams and illustrations that are not original have been used with proper attribution and credit to their respective sources.

If you believe that any content in this book infringes upon your copyright or trademark, please contact us immediately at support@gitforgits.com. Upon notification, corrective action will be taken promptly.

Prologue

The inspiration for this book stems from observing skilled professionals who, despite their expertise, encounter challenges due to memory lapses during exams. My objective was to develop a concise, exam-focused resource that would enable users to swiftly access the information they require. My approach is focused on presenting each abbreviation as a trigger that produces a practical image, rather than an abstract line in a glossary. When you encounter an acronym in this book, you should understand its meaning in the context of the control architecture, along with a brief explanation of its relevance to operations and exam items.

The content has been organised around five operational domains that mirror the SY0-701 objectives and everyday security responsibilities. Each domain contains key references, crosswalks and short scenarios to facilitate rehearsal of connections rather than isolated facts. In order to assist you with finding terms quickly during last-minute revision, I have included printable cheat sheets and an indexed spreadsheet. To facilitate this process, practice items are designed to pair acronyms with their respective appearances in multiple-choice questions, thereby training recognition in context.

I expect you to use this book actively. The process involves reading a domain, answering a few paired items, and then taking a timed mini-exam to test recall under pressure. Please use the provided cheat sheets to prepare for the test. These will help us to revise key concepts and understand the theory behind the practice. I concentrated on clarity: concise entries, one specific example, and explicit cross-references that demonstrate how controls interact when incidents escalate.

This whole approach enables the refinement of mental models rather than the mere memorisation of unrelated terms.

The objective of this book is to ensure that the final days are managed efficiently with confidence, and to demonstrate practical command as soon as operations resume.

How to use this book?

You're not here just to flip pages, we are here to own every acronym in your memory. Pick any acronym, point to it, and explain out loud what it means, why it matters, and how you'd use it in a real-world scenario. Spot a term you can't immediately define? Circle it, jot it on your phone, then teach it back before you move on. Short bursts of this self-quizzing, during your coffee break or while waiting for a colleague, turn downtime into high-value study sessions that cement these concepts in your mind.

You'll find scenario-based questions after each subtopic. Treat them as mini simulations: read the question, imagine we are in that situation, and answer without peeking at the definitions. When you get stuck, flip back, review the entry, then answer again. Keep a "focus list" of three to five acronyms that challenge you most, and revisit those daily until you can define and apply each one confidently.

Balance depth with variety by rotating across the five parts in each study session. After covering five to ten acronyms, close the book and write down everything you remember. Compare your notes to the original entries and celebrate how few you miss. Spacing these quick reviews throughout your day, rather than doing one long cram, locks knowledge into long-term memory. Before you know it, recalling any term under exam pressure will feel as natural as breathing. Good luck, your mastery starts here, one acronym at a time.

Content

Preface

If we are getting ready for the SY0-701 exam and need some last-minute study material, this CompTIA Security+ Last Minute Revision guide is just what you need. It's a concise, fast-paced reference book that'll help us get up to speed. Over 400 acronyms and explanations are included, all mapped directly to the five exam domains including:

- General Security Concepts
- Threats, Vulnerabilities and Mitigations
- Security Architecture
- Security Operations, and
- Security Program Management and Oversight

This book focuses on recalling things when we are feeling pressured. Every term or concept has a definition and a practical context, so you can remember an acronym while we are answering scenario questions. It's really easy to find what we are looking for in these quick cross-references, which link related controls, protocols and frameworks. It'll help us convert short-term memory into judgment that's ready for the exam. There are printable cheat sheets and an indexed Excel file to help us look stuff up super quickly when we are revising at the last minute.

This concise companion helps sharpen recall, connect concepts and approach exam day with clear focus. Inside, you get quick crosswalks between exam objectives and operational tasks, mnemonics for retention, and a printable A3 cheat sheet with references.

So, how do you use it?

Just flip to the domain you need to reinforce, read the related cheat sheet, then answer a short practice set. You can use the Excel index to find a term in seconds. Then run through the mock exam to time your recall and adjust your focus.

Who should use this book?

This book is for security professionals who've already got experience under their belts and are ready to put the finishing touches on their certification. And, if you like short, practical examples over long, boring prose, you will enjoy this one too. Even the instructors who need a compact classroom handout keep asking for such a book.

GitforGits

Prerequisites

This book has been designed for security professionals who already have a solid foundation of experience and are preparing to finalise their certification. If you prefer concise, practical examples to extensive descriptions, you will find this book engaging.

Codes Usage

Are you in need of some helpful code examples to assist you in your programming and documentation? Look no further! Our book offers a wealth of supplemental material, including code examples and exercises.

Not only is this book here to aid you in getting your job done, but you have our permission to use the example code in your programs and documentation. However, please note that if you are reproducing a significant portion of the code, we do require you to contact us for permission.

But don't worry, using several chunks of code from this book in your program or answering a question by citing our book and quoting example code does not require permission. But if you do choose to give credit, an attribution typically includes the title, author, publisher, and ISBN. For example, " CompTIA Security+ Last Minute Revision by Xandar Pelin".

If you are unsure whether your intended use of the code examples falls under fair use or the permissions outlined above, please do not hesitate to reach out to us at support@gitforgits.com.

We are happy to assist and clarify any concerns.

Acknowledgement

I owe a tremendous debt of gratitude to GitforGits, for their unflagging enthusiasm and wise counsel throughout the entire process of writing this book. Their knowledge and careful editing helped make sure the piece was useful for people of all reading levels and comprehension skills. In addition, I'd like to thank everyone involved in the publishing process for their efforts in making this book a reality. Their efforts, from copyediting to advertising, made the project what it is today.

About Security+ (V7) Exam

This section orients you to what the CompTIA Security+ SY0-701 assessment measures, how the test is delivered, and what real-world skills you will be expected to demonstrate. The wording below is adapted from the official CompTIA exam objectives so you have a compact, exam-ready reference. The official objectives documented by CompTIA is available to download from the link: ***https://github.com/kittenpub/comptia_securityplus_v7***

Validation by the exam:

You will be tested on your ability to:

- Assess an enterprise security posture and recommend practical defenses.
- Monitor and secure hybrid environments that include cloud, mobile, and IoT assets.
- Operate with awareness of applicable regulations, governance, risk and compliance responsibilities.
- Identify, analyze, and respond to security events and incidents.

Accreditation and development:

The Security+ exam is ANSI-accredited to align with ISO 17024 standards.

The team at CompTIA updates the objectives through industry subject-matter expert workshops and wide surveys to reflect employer expectations and operational realities.

Test details (quick facts):

Exam number: SY0-701.

Maximum questions: 90.

Question formats: Multiple-choice and performance-based items.

Time allowed: 90 minutes.

Domain breakdown (weighting):

General Security Concepts - 12%

Threats, Vulnerabilities, and Mitigations - 22%

Security Architecture - 18%

Security Operations - 28%

Security Program Management and Oversight - 20%

These above percentages indicate the relative emphasis across the exam and should shape how you allocate last-minute review time.

How to use this chapter:

The domain weighting is there to help us prioritise short review passes. Just read each domain's learning objectives, then test yourself with the paired practice items in this volume.

PART I: GENERAL SECURITY CONCEPTS

Authentication & Access Control

It's all about making sure who you are is who you say you are, and that we are allowed to do what you say you are allowed to do. Authentication is like the first gate where MFA or 2FA proves who you are, often using something you know, something you have, or something you are. These days, most people use FIDO2 tokens and TOTP instead of weaker PAP methods. Once you've got the identity sorted, AAA systems take care of authorisation and accounting. RADIUS or TACACS+ handle network access, and RBAC makes it easy to grant permissions when we need to.

And, access control lists are still useful at the network and file level to enforce rules, while PSK and PEAP are used in wireless access scenarios where credential protection matters. When it comes to device ownership models like BYOD, COPE, COBO and CYOD, things are changing. We're seeing stricter controls on corporate devices, and personal devices are now requiring conditional access and MDM. In cloud environments, IAMaaS and SCIM automate provisioning and deprovisioning, and SPIFFE with SPIRE provide workload identities for service-to-service authentication. And logging and audit trails complete the loop so accounting can show who accessed which resource and when. We can use guardrails like CSPM to spot misconfigurations that could let identities access things they shouldn't.

There are DNS privacy protocols like DoH and DoT that affect how resolvers fit into access paths. We make sure these elements are all working together so that when we log in, the identity is linked to the right role and the right rules, and everything is recorded so that the system stays strong and follows the rules.

2FA

Two-Factor Authentication

When we're looking at ways to check someone's identity, we'll think about two-factor authentication. It pairs something we know (a password) with something we have (a smartphone app or hardware token) or something we are (a fingerprint). In banking, customers prove who they are with 2FA before approving big transfers, which cuts down on fraudulent withdrawals. When we set up 2FA on a VPN portal, we first enter the password, then supply a time-based one-time code generated on the device. The security teams make sure that 2FA is part of the admin consoles, so that financial-grade protection is in place. We need to keep this "double lock" approach in mind whenever we're designing access controls that need to stop credential stuffing and phishing attacks.

AAA

Authentication, Authorization, Accounting

There are three phases to the AAA, and it's useful to understand these to get the head around layered access control. The authentication just makes sure that we are who we say we are by checking the credentials or certificates. The authorization checks what we can do by looking at the rules in the directory service. And the accounting records every activity, login attempt, resource access and configuration change in audit trails for analysis. It's used by telecom providers to measure how much prepaid data people use, and by businesses to control access to cloud services through VPNs and firewalls. When we are setting up AAA, it's important to make sure that each session follows a clear path. This means that it first identifies the user, then permits the action, and then records the event for compliance or forensics.

ACL

Access Control List

What if we were in charge of a private event where only invited guests could get in? An ACL does the same thing in network and file system contexts. The router uses ACL rules to allow or block traffic based on the source IP, destination port and protocol. The file server enforces ACL entries that specify which users can read, write or execute critical documents. These translate ACLs into security group rules, which help to isolate workloads by environment. So, when we are trying to sort out connectivity issues, we check the ACL hit counters to see which rule allowed or denied each packet.

AUP

Acceptable Use Policy

AUP stands for Acceptable Use Policy, and it's basically like a class rules thing for technology use. It tells us what we are allowed to do, what apps are approved, how we should handle network resources and data, and it bans activities like sharing personal files or using cloud storage without permission. In healthcare, AUPs say that clinical staff shouldn't install personal chat apps on patient-care workstations. If there's a security incident, investigators refer to the AUP to see if a user's broken any rules. It's a good idea to get the staff involved in regular AUP reviews during onboarding and refresher training. A clear, user-friendly AUP is a great way to reduce insider risks by setting expectations from the start and guiding everyone towards safe, compliant behaviours in the organisation.

BYOD

Bring Your Own Device

When the organisation lets employees use their own devices for work, people use their phones or laptops. It's all about implementing mobile-device management profiles that enforce encryption, screen locks and remote-wipe capabilities before allowing network access. The network team puts BYOD traffic into separate VLANs and runs health checks via NAC so that if any devices get compromised, they can't reach the critical servers. A good BYOD programme can help staff get more done, make it easier for them to access emails and work together using the tools they like. The tricky bit is striking a balance between making things easy for users and making sure the rules are being followed and that everything is being monitored all the time.

COBO

Corporate-Owned, Business-Only

A COBO model means the organisation provides hardware that's just for business functions. The company provides tablets with productivity and analytics apps already on them, but we can't install any of the own software. The endpoint teams make sure that patch cycles, disk encryption and application whitelisting are all set up the same way on every COBO device. Its EDR solution is all about corporate workloads, making it super accurate. As asset inventories only show managed hardware, it makes reporting compliance easier. And for high-security environments, trading desks or government facilities, COBO is the way to go. It gets rid of any risks from personal use and makes sure everything's set up the same way. COBO keeps personal and business functions separate, so the devices are protected from malware and unauthorised software.

COPE

Corporate-Owned, Personally Enabled

With the COPE approach, we use a company-owned smartphone or laptop that supports both work and personal activities. It's a secure container for corporate apps, and it encrypts business data separately from personal files. If we leave the company or lose a device, security teams can remotely wipe only the corporate container, keeping the personal photos and messages safe. As for mobile app management, this makes sure that antivirus updates and patches are applied within the company. This balanced model gives us productivity tools and personal flexibility, while keeping sensitive information under control and stopping shadow IT.

CYOD

Choose Your Own Device

The IT department has put together a list of approved device models for us to choose from. It's a simple process where we pick a laptop or smartphone that ticks the boxes, and then we get it with all the necessary security settings, disk encryption, endpoint protection and apps already on it. The procurement team benefits from volume licensing on the approved list, while the support teams manage a limited hardware portfolio. And we can enjoy device choice without compromising security, with consistent patching and compliance across every CYOD endpoint. This approach makes it easier to get things up and running, cuts down on help-desk calls and keeps security standards across the board high.

MFA

Multifactor Authentication

The MFA adds layers like biometrics, hardware keys and contextual analytics to strengthen identity verification. When we sign into a privileged console, the system might ask us to scan the fingerprint and enter a one-time code that'll be sent to we as a push notification. Then there are risk-based engines, which check things like session attributes, device type, location or behavioural patterns. These only add extra factors when they think something is a bit dodgy. When we integrate with PAM solutions, it makes sure that MFA is on for admin-level access to servers and cloud resources. The adaptive design of MFA helps us keep security and usability, which is important for protecting the digital assets and meeting strict rules and regulations.

PAP

Password Authentication Protocol

In some older VPNs and legacy PPP links, PAP sends user credentials in cleartext, which leaves them exposed to eavesdroppers. When we audit network traffic and spot PAP exchanges, we treat them as high-risk findings. The plan is to put PAP inside an IPsec tunnel or upgrade endpoints to CHAP or EAP alternatives that encrypt credentials. You'll need to keep track of any remaining PAP usage and plan for phased retirements to stronger protocols. And if we get how the PAP doesn't do encryption, you'll know how to make sure we have got secure authentication solutions in places where we have got modern and old systems all mixed.

PEAP

Protected Extensible Authentication Protocol

Enterprise Wi-Fi lets us do this by creating a secure tunnel using something called PEAP, which hides the login details from anyone trying to attack you. The wireless team installs server certificates on access points and end-user devices, enabling mutual TLS authentication. The PEAP is often used with MSCHAPv2 for inner authentication, and it keeps usernames and passwords safe on corporate and guest networks. We keep an eye on the TLS-tunnel health and certificate validity to stop any connectivity issues. The fact that PEAP works well with most operating systems and network hardware makes it a good choice for setting up on a whole campus, as it reduces the risk of credential theft.

PSK

Pre-Shared Key

In small-office or branch-network setups, the PSK makes it easy to secure Wi-Fi or IPsec tunnels.

We usually share a passphrase, usually through the secure user portal, so that devices can work out the encryption keys. We rotate PSKs regularly and track device fingerprints to detect unauthorised use. The network dashboard will let us know if someone tries to connect with a revoked key. Although PSK management isn't the best solution for big companies, it's still handy for smaller environments where manual distribution and regular rotation are enough to keep things secure.

RADIUS

Remote Authentication Dial-In User Service

For centralised access management, RADIUS handles AAA requests from network devices. It's like, when we connect to the company Wi-Fi or a VPN, the network gear sends the details to the RADIUS server, which then checks the identity against LDAP or Active Directory. The server gives us policy attributes that set VLAN IDs, session timeouts and bandwidth quotas. And the accounting logs record when sessions start and stop, which is great for planning and billing. Then we tweak the retry intervals and timeout settings on RADIUS clients to strike a balance between keeping things resilient against brute-force attempts. Its scalability and extensibility make it a must for large, heterogeneous network environments.

RBAC

Role-Based Access Control

RBAC is great for assigning access rights to roles instead of individual users when we are designing permission models. We define roles, like "Finance Analyst" or "DevOps Engineer", and map permissions for data, apps or systems to these roles. It's all based on the role we are assigned, so it's simple to keep track of changes in personnel. The global enterprises use RBAC to make sure that new hires get the exact access needed for their jobs straight away, and that departures automatically lose those rights. Just think of RBAC as job title badges that unlock only the doors we need. When we use RBAC in Active Directory or cloud IAM platforms, we make sure that users only have the minimum permissions they need, which reduces the risk of over-permissioned accounts.

TACACS+

Terminal Access Controller Access-Control System Plus

If we need to be very precise about who can access network devices, TACACS+ separates the steps of authentication (verifying the user is who they say they are), authorisation (making sure the user is allowed to access what they need) and accounting (tracking the user's activity) into separate steps. The routers and switches send login attempts to a TACACS+ server. The server checks the user's credentials, then decides which commands the user can run, and finally records everything the user does. These days, big service providers use TACACS+ to set different levels of access for engineers, depending on whether they need to make changes to the configuration or just monitor the devices. Because TACACS+ encrypts everything, not just the password, we can be sure that sensitive command streams cannot be intercepted. To put it simply, TACACS+ is like a security guard. It checks the ID, confirms which rooms we can enter, and notes down every corridor we go through.

CSPM

Cloud Security Posture Management

As the organisation moves its data to the cloud, CSPM regularly checks the settings to make sure they meet the best standards. The CSPM tools connect to cloud accounts. They scan storage buckets, networking rules and IAM policies. They flag any problems, like misconfigurations, S3 buckets that are publicly exposed or overly permissive roles. This helps to stop attackers from exploiting them. People who work in security use CSPM to automate fixing problems or to show that they are following the rules. We can see a record of this in dashboards, which show when someone has accidentally disabled encryption.

DoH

DNS over HTTPS

Whenever we make DNS queries, a feature called DoH puts them inside standard HTTPS requests. This means that they are protected from network eavesdroppers. We can set up the browsers or DNS resolvers to use DoH endpoints. This means that people with bad intentions on public Wi-Fi can't see the websites we are visiting. This means that companies need to balance privacy and security. If we only use DoH, the firewalls won't be able to see DNS traffic. To do this, we use special proxies that are managed by the company. These proxies decrypt and filter DNS queries in the cloud. DoH is like a locked, anonymous courier envelope that hides the contents from prying eyes.

DoT

DNS over TLS

Just like DoH, DoT keeps DNS lookups safe by wrapping them in a special TLS channel on port 853. When we set up DoT on resolvers, we split DNS encryption from web traffic, which keeps network monitoring working and makes firewall rules easier. The security appliances can check or block DNS queries before TLS termination, which makes sure the policy is enforced. Service providers often offer DoT endpoints for their enterprise customers, which let us route DNS through trusted channels. To put it simply, DoT is like a private phone line to the DNS server. The questions travel in a private call, safe from interception, while still passing through the organisation's monitoring centre.

FIDO2

Fast IDentity Online 2

It's all about phishing-resistant authentication these days, and FIDO2 is the name on everyone's lips. It swaps out shared secrets for asymmetric cryptography, which is cool. We can register a FIDO2 authenticator, a USB security key or a platform-embedded TPM against the online account. When we log in, the server gives us a challenge to sign with a private key, which proves we own the device without sending reusable passwords. So, businesses are using FIDO2 with their single-sign-on portals, right? That means their employees can either tap a hardware key or use Windows Hello facial recognition. Basically, it's like a personalised padlock that only we can open with the own unique key. This makes credential theft pretty much impossible and makes it harder for attackers.

IAMaaS

Identity and Access Management as a Service

Using cloud-hosted IAM means we get a third-party to take care of the directory infrastructure, single sign-on and multifactor flows. It's a piece of cake to connect applications, SaaS tools, custom APIs or on-premises services to the IAMaaS platform, and we can centralise user lifecycles and consent flows without buying hardware. And security teams use the built-in analytics to spot unusual logins, and they work with provisioning protocols like SCIM. It's basically like a managed concierge service that hands out digital keys, tracks usage and revokes access when staff change roles. So, we don't have to worry about scaling directory servers or patching identity-management software.

SCIM

System for Cross-Domain Identity Management

Whether we are onboarding or offboarding users, SCIM makes account provisioning between identity providers and target applications a breeze. It's all about making sure that when someone joins, all their details, like name, email and what groups they're in, automatically pop into the HR system, cloud apps and collaboration platforms. When they leave, SCIM triggers deprovisioning processes, making sure stale accounts are disabled everywhere. The security teams use SCIM to keep things consistent and reduce the number of "orphaned" accounts, which can be a risk from the inside. SCIM is like a conveyor belt that moves user data between systems without any manual steps or human errors.

SPIFFE

Secure Production Identity Framework for Everyone

SPIFFE is great for managing microservices in dynamic environments, as it provides workload identities that aren't tied to IPs or hostnames. Basically, we integrate SPIFFE libraries into services so that each one gets a cryptographic identity document at runtime. And with mutual TLS between workloads, we can have secure service-to-service authentication without having to deal with manual certificate management. So, cloud-native teams use SPIFFE to automate trust chains across Kubernetes clusters, VMs and serverless functions. To put it simply, SPIFFE is like an automated notary service. Every service has its own ID card, and other services accept it without needing preconfigured IP lists or DNS entries.

SPIRE

SPIFFE Runtime Environment

SPIRE oversees orchestrating things when we are using SPIFFE standards in production, and it automatically issues and rotates workload identities. All we must do is deploy SPIRE servers and agents across the infrastructure, and the agents will request workload certificates from the server and renew them before they expire. The side-car proxies or service meshes use these certificates to set up mTLS connections. Its plugin architecture lets us integrate with various orchestration platforms, Kubernetes, Nomad or VMs, maintaining a unified identity layer. At SPIRE, we're like the behind-the-scenes team for SPIFFE, taking care of the certificate lifecycles so that the services always show valid, trusted IDs without any manual intervention.

Knowledge Check

1. Which two technologies provide encrypted DNS lookups?

A. ACL + RBAC
B. DoH + DoT
C. PAP + PEAP
D. PSK + RADIUS

2. Which pair represents a service that centralizes AAA functions and the protocol that secures Wi-Fi by tunneling initial credentials?

A. RADIUS + PEAP
B. TACACS+ + 2FA
C. SCIM + COPE
D. FIDO2 + MFA

3. Which combination enforces least-privilege through role assignments and logs all access attempts for auditing?

A. RBAC + AAA
B. BYOD + AUP

C. SPIFFE + SPIRE
D. CSPM + IAMaaS

4. Which two approaches involve corporate devices with either no personal use or limited personal use?
   A. COBO + COPE
   B. CYOD + PAP
   C. ACL + AUP
   D. MFA + 2FA

5. Which pair are multifactor authentication standards, one focusing on hardware tokens and the other on adaptive factors?
   A. FIDO2 + MFA
   B. PEAP + PAP
   C. DoH + DoT
   D. SCIM + SPIRE

6. Which duo automates workload identity issuance in dynamic cloud-native environments?
   A. SPIFFE + SPIRE
   B. RADIUS + Tacacs+
   C. PSK + PAP
   D. COPE + CYOD

7. Which pair describes user provisioning automation and cloud-hosted identity management?
   A. SCIM + IAMaaS
   B. AAA + ACL
   C. BYOD + COB0
   D. AUP + RADIUS

8. Which technologies together deliver device-based authentication and shared-secret encryption for small offices?
   A. PSK + FIDO2
   B. RADIUS + TACACS+
   C. PAP + PEAP
   D. COPE + CYOD

9. Which two ensure modern multifactor access while still supporting legacy cleartext authentication methods?
   A. 2FA + PAP
   B. DoH + DoT
   C. RBAC + AUP
   D. CSPM + SPIFFE

10. Which pair integrates corporate policy enforcement for user behavior and network-access governance?
    A. AUP + ACL
    B. RADIUS + DoH
    C. SCIM + SPIRE
    D. CYOD + 2FA

Answer Key:

1. B
2. A
3. A
4. A
5. A
6. A
7. A
8. A
9. A
10. A

Cryptographic Foundation & Key Management

It's all about keeping secrets safe and giving us the tools to prove those secrets haven't been tampered with. A symmetric cipher like AES or AES-256 gives us fast confidentiality for disks and tunnels, while an asymmetric algorithm like RSA or ECC helps us establish trust and exchange keys without sharing secrets directly. If we look at TLS handshakes, you'll see ECDHE or DHE being used to provide perfect forward secrecy, and ECDSA being used to sign certificates so we can verify who issued them. These days, TLS setups tend to go for AEAD ciphers like GCM, which mix confidentiality and integrity. And HMAC is still a great way to make sure messages are authentic when keys are shared.

When we need tamper-resistant storage, you'll be using a KMS or an HSM to manage the keys. A PKI made up of CAs and an RA issues certificates; OCSP and CRL provide revocation checks so that if a key's been compromised it stops working. You'll be working with keystores in JKS or PFX formats and using PKCS#11 APIs when integrating hardware tokens. Passwords need slow hashing, so PBKDF2 or better functions protect credentials from brute force. PGP still works for secure email and signing artifacts. It's best to avoid legacy algorithms like DES, 3DES and MD5, as they don't stand up to modern attack tests.

You'll be practising key rotation, making sure keys don't last too long and planning recovery with key escrow only when the policy says we need to. Mutual TLS, or mTLS, is a simple, strong pattern for service-to-service identity. When we put these elements together, we can choose the right cipher, the right storage, and the right lifecycle for keys, so cryptography actually protects the systems we run.

3DES

Triple Data Encryption Standard

This was introduced to make DES last longer, and 3DES uses the original DES cipher three times with multiple keys in an "encrypt-decrypt-encrypt" sequence. When they were switching to stronger algorithms, financial institutions adopted 3DES to protect ATM PINs and transaction records. For legacy payment platforms where AES isn't supported, 3DES is a fallback option. Most of the time, performance benchmarking shows higher CPU usage and latency compared to modern ciphers, so 3DES is only used when compatibility is a priority over efficiency.

AES

Advanced Encryption Standard

Everyone knows that AES is the go-to symmetric cipher. It secures everything from disk volumes to TLS channels. If we are using hardware acceleration, like Intel's AES-NI, we can encrypt data blocks quickly. This is great for high-throughput environments like VPN gateways and database clusters. If we configure AES in GCM mode, we can combine encryption with integrity checks in a single operation, which makes development easier and reduces attack surface. The AES is the go-to choice for building encrypted storage or communication systems because it's got the thumbs-up from the government and is under the microscope of the community.

AES-256

Advanced Encryption Standard 256-Bit

When it's important to keep things secret, AES-256 is the go-to with its 256-bit key, making it super tough to break. We've got the best cloud key management services and HSM appliances out there, so we can generate, store and rotate AES-256 keys without any hassle. It's often used in high-security areas like defence, finance and healthcare, for both data storage and when it's being sent from one place to another. While larger keys do have a slightly negative impact on performance, modern CPU instruction sets have come a long way in minimising this, meaning we can deliver robust encryption without sacrificing responsiveness.

DES

Data Encryption Standard

In the 70s, the US government started using DES, a cryptographic pioneer, for things like securing data and communications. It's a good example of a Feistel network and key scheduling. The 56-bit key length that was once secure is now easily broken in a few hours on regular hardware. These days, if there's even the slightest hint of DES in network or storage setups, we jump on it straight away. If we look at how DES works and what its weak spots are, you'll get a better idea of why AES and 3DES became so popular.

DHE

Diffie-Hellman Ephemeral

Enabling DHE in the TLS configuration makes perfect forward secrecy a reality, generating fresh Diffie-Hellman parameters for each handshake. All the big messaging platforms and financial systems use DHE to stop people decrypting messages retrospectively, even if long-term server keys leak. It's important to keep an eye on how well the handshake is performing, as bigger DH parameter sizes can cause a noticeable delay. If we get how ephemeral key exchanges work, we can set up secure channels that protect past communications against future hacks.

ECC

Elliptic Curve Cryptography

For environments where space is at a premium, mobile apps, IoT devices and embedded systems, ECC provides strong public-key security with much smaller keys compared to RSA. Nowadays, Curve25519 and P-256 are pretty much everywhere, offering a great balance between performance and security. When we use library calls for ECC-based TLS or SSH, we get shorter handshake times and less bandwidth. If we know the way around elliptic curve math, we can pick the right curves and parameters for the organisation's risk and performance needs.

ECDHE

Elliptic Curve Diffie-Hellman Ephemeral

ECDHE is the backbone of modern TLS handshakes, combining ECC's efficiency with the security of ephemeral keys. The high-traffic APIs and microservices prefer ECDHE ciphersuites to make sure that data remains secret and that the system doesn't take too long to respond. If we want to enable ECDHE in the server configurations, you'll need to select compatible curves (like X25519) and update client support matrices. And if we have got ECDHE down, we can be sure that each connection session is protected, even against attackers who might compromise long-term keys later.

ECDSA

Elliptic Curve Digital Signature Algorithm

The software's useful for things like signature size and verification speed, blockchain transactions and certificate issuance. If we sign with ECDSA, you'll get compact signatures that keep the certificate chain from getting bloated in TLS, and verification operations will still be faster than RSA at the same security level. It integrates with PKI platforms and code-signing pipelines to use ECDSA for non-repudiation without overloading constrained devices. If we understand ECDSA's parameter choices and trust anchors, you'll be well placed to design lean, secure signature schemes.

HMAC

Hashed Message Authentication Code

HMAC is a cool way to make sure the data is both legit and secure in those symmetric-key setups. It basically takes these hash functions like SHA-256 and pairs them with a secret key. Basically, we embed HMAC values in API request headers, which means servers can verify that payloads haven't been tampered with and originate from trusted clients. If we automate HMAC secret rotation in the key management system, we can stop stale keys from undermining security. It's easy to design secure messaging protocols and defend webhook integrations against replay or forgery attacks just by understanding how HMAC works.

IDEA

International Data Encryption Algorithm

Heading outside the AES-centric world, IDEA offers a 128-bit key block cipher based on modular arithmetic and XOR operations. Although AES has pretty much replaced it, we still come across IDEA in some VPN setups that haven't been updated, and in a few specialist encryption products. If we look at how it's structured and the history of its patents, we can get a better idea of the trade-offs involved in cipher design. If we know about IDEA's place in cryptographic evolution, we can evaluate bespoke or proprietary algorithms better when legacy compatibility or specific security properties are required.

MD5

Message Digest 5

MD5 is still used as a quick checksum tool. It generates 128-bit hashes for file integrity verification, ISO images and software packages. But collision attacks mean MD5 isn't suitable for cryptographic authentication. If security checks highlight MD5 in certificates or password hashes, plan to switch to SHA-2 or SHA-3 straight away. And studying MD5's weaknesses can tell us a lot about how hashes have evolved and what modern algorithms need to be able to do to stop collision and preimage threats.

PBKDF2

Password-Based Key Derivation Function 2

The process of turning a simple password into a cryptographic key uses something called PBKDF2's iterative hashing process. These days, security architects are using PBKDF2 to store user passwords in password-storage systems, often within application frameworks or identity stores. This means that the passwords go through thousands of hash rounds before they're stored. So, compromised databases can't be attacked offline with a brute-force attack because each guess uses a lot of CPUs. The cloud-based identity services we use here use PBKDF2 parameters, iteration count and salt length in the configuration profiles. If we know about PBKDF2 settings, we can work out the right balance between how long it takes to use the system and how well it can withstand attacks. This is important for any system that handles sensitive information.

PGP

Pretty Good Privacy

For end-to-end email and file transfers, we often use PGP's hybrid model, which uses both public-key and symmetric cryptography. The users generate PGP key pairs and share public keys via key servers or by swapping them directly. When a sender encrypts a message, PGP selects a random symmetric session key to encrypt the payload, then wraps that key with the recipient's public key. The recipient software then decrypts the session key with their private key, and the message is recovered. If we understand how PGP works, we can set up secure email solutions and verify digital signatures in cross-organisational communication.

PKCS

Public Key Cryptography Standards

The PKCS is a set of standards that RSA Laboratories helped to develop. It defines data formats and protocols for key exchange, certificate requests (PKCS#10), token storage (PKCS#12) and cryptographic operations. People who develop and integrate systems use PKCS specifications when they generate CSRs, package private keys and certificates into PFX files or interface with hardware tokens. If we follow the PKCS guidelines, we can make sure the software works with other libraries, OpenSSL, BouncyCastle, and hardware modules.

PKI

Public Key Infrastructure

The way we communicate digitally depends on a strong PKI. A PKI issues, renews and revokes X.509 certificates through hierarchical trust chains anchored at a root CA. Then there are the Certificate Authorities, who run registration authorities (RAs) to check identity documents before issuing certificates. Lots of companies use internal PKIs to secure VPNs, Wi-Fi and internal applications, and they often work with HSMs to protect keys. A good way to manage the PKI is to publish CRLs or enable OCSP responders for real-time revocation checks. If we understand the principles of PKI design, we can create a certificate lifecycle that is both secure and easy to use.

RA

Registration Authority

In a PKI, the RA is like the gatekeeper for issuing certificates. So, the admin workflows route CSR submissions to the RA, who verify the applicant's identity using digital or physical documentation. Then, the RA forwards the requests that have been validated to the CA. The idea is to integrate RAs into identity-proofing portals and help-desk ticketing systems, which should ensure a documented audit trail for every certificate. If we set up automated RA processes with configurable approval rules, we can get certificates issued more quickly while staying on the right side of the rules. If we know about RA functions, we can design secure enrollment workflows that balance operational speed with thorough identity checks.

RSA

Rivest–Shamir–Adleman

RSA is one of the first practical public-key algorithms. It's used for securing key exchanges and digital signatures using modular exponentiation with large prime numbers. Typically, web servers use RSA certificates with 2048- or 4096-bit keys to set up secure TLS sessions, and document signing tools use RSA for non-repudiation. The best high-performance systems use optimisations based on the Chinese Remainder Theorem and hardware acceleration. When it comes to RSA key management, it's all about keeping those private keys super safe in HSMs or encrypted keystores. If we can get the head around RSA's maths and how it works, we can pick the right key sizes and deployment platforms for the job.

SHA

Secure Hash Algorithm

A family of cryptographic hash functions, SHA-1, SHA-2 (SHA-224, SHA-256, SHA-384, SHA-512) and SHA-3, produces fixed-length digests to verify data integrity. Software distribution pipelines attach SHA digests to released binaries, so users can confirm downloads haven't been tampered with. Version control systems and container registries use something called SHA hashes to identify immutable artifacts. Security policies say that we need to move from SHA-1 (which is now vulnerable to collisions) to SHA-2 or SHA-3. Mastering SHA variants means we can use the right function for checksums, digital signatures and HMAC operations across different applications.

SSL

Secure Sockets Layer

One of the first ways of encrypting web traffic, SSL got the ball rolling on encrypted client-server communication. The versions 2.0 and 3.0 have had known vulnerabilities, POODLE, BEAST, and have been replaced by TLS. If we know the stuff when it comes to SSL, it can help us out when we are doing audits or threat assessments and we come across legacy devices that are still advertising that they support SSL. If we can see where SSL is weak, we can plan to move to TLS-only set-ups. It also shows how important it is to turn off old ciphers.

TLS

Transport Layer Security

TLS is the modern standard for secure communications, and it's evolved from SSL. The versions 1.2 and 1.3 define how to negotiate cipher suites, AES-GCM, ECDHE key exchanges and HMAC or AEAD constructions. It's used in web servers, APIs and email systems to make sure everything is secure and private. We can set TLS parameters, protocol versions, cipher priorities and certificate verification via server settings or load-balancer profiles.

JKS

Java KeyStore

Any apps built on the Java platform store their cryptographic keys and certificates in JKS files. It's developers' job to load JKS keystores into Java Runtime Environment configurations, Tomcat, Spring Boot or application servers to configure HTTPS connectors or sign JAR files. And the **`keytool`** utility is great for managing JKS entries, importing certificates, generating CSRs and setting alias passwords. If we know about the JKS format and how to move things over to PKCS#12 keystores, we can keep the Java setups secure and work with enterprise CAs.

KMS

Key Management Service

Services like cloud and on-premises Key Management Services offer centralised storage of encryption keys, lifecycle automation and cryptographic operations via APIs. We can provision keys, define usage policies and trigger automatic rotation schedules. When we use applications, they ask for data encryption or digital-signature operations by calling KMS endpoints. These make sure that keys never leave secure hardware or virtual enclaves. And KMS integration makes compliance reporting easier and reduces operational overhead for key custody. If we understand the features of KMS, we can create key-centric security models that scale across services and regions.

PFX

Personal Information Exchange

An PFX (PKCS#12) file is a single, password-protected archive that bundles private keys, public certificates and certificate-chain certificates. If we are using Windows certificate import wizards or any of the many development frameworks out there, you'll find that PFX is great for SSL/TLS configuration. Then we generate PFX files from CSRs and HSM exports, and get them to web servers or application services securely. And if we manage PFX passphrases and storage permissions, we can be sure that only authorised processes can decrypt and load critical keys.

PKCS#11

The PKCS#11 standard defines a standard API, Cryptoki, for interacting with cryptographic tokens such as HSMs and smart cards. It's used by applications to generate keys, perform digital-signature operations and store certificates within secure hardware. Then we have got middleware vendors, who provide PKCS#11 drivers to integrate HSM appliances with enterprise software, web servers, VPN gateways and code-signing tools. But if we know the stuff with PKCS#11, we can build high-assurance solutions that keep keys separate from the host operating system, meeting some stringent security requirements.

mTLS

Mutual TLS

Simply put, mutual TLS extends standard TLS by requiring both client and server to present valid certificates, enabling two-way authentication. The way API gateways and service meshes work is that they adopt mTLS to verify service and user identities before granting access, so we don't have to rely on bearer tokens alone. So, configuration basically means creating client certificates, distributing them safely and updating trust stores on both sides.

Knowledge Check

1. Which two provide perfect forward secrecy in TLS handshakes?

A. DES + 3DES

B. DHE + ECDHE
C. SHA + MD5
D. RSA + ECC

2. Which pair represents symmetric block ciphers used for bulk data encryption?
A. RSA + ECDSA
B. DES + 3DES
C. PBKDF2 + HMAC
D. PGP + PKI

3. Which two are cryptographic hash functions?
A. MD5 + SHA
B. AES + AES-256
C. IDEA + RSA
D. SSL + TLS

4. Which combination consists of public-key algorithms?
A. RSA + ECC
B. HMAC + PBKDF2
C. DES + AES
D. JKS + KMS

5. Which duo are digital signature schemes?
A. ECDSA + RSA
B. MD5 + HMAC
C. PFX + PKCS#11
D. DHE + PBKDF2

6. Which two handle key derivation and management in modern systems?
A. PBKDF2 + KMS
B. ECC + ECDHE
C. SSL + mTLS
D. JKS + RA

7. Which pair defines formats for bundling private keys and certificates?
A. PFX + PKCS
B. AES + 3DES
C. SHA + MD5
D. DHE + TLS

8. Which two APIs or stores integrate with hardware security modules?
A. PKCS#11 + JKS

B. DES + IDEA
C. RSA + ECC
D. HMAC + PBKDF2

9. Which combination covers standard TLS/SSL protocols?
A. SSL + TLS
B. PGP + PKI
C. AES-256 + 3DES
D. DHE + ECC

10. Which duo ensures mutual authentication between client and server?
A. SSL + SHA
B. TLS + mTLS
C. AES + DES
D. ECDSA + IDEA

Answer Key:

1. B

2. B

3. A

4. A

5. A

6. A

7. A

8. A

9. A

10. B

Security Services & Network Protocols

In the world of modern systems, network traffic is like the blood that keeps everything running, and the protocols that handle it are the rules that govern how we communicate and the potential risks. TCP/IP provides reliable delivery for most services, while UDP supports low-latency use cases. There's a lot to take in, but understanding both of these is key to placing controls where they matter. All that hypertext traffic goes over HTTP and its secure version, HTTPS, which relies on TLS for confidentiality and integrity. The Domain Name System (DNS) is how domains are resolved, and the Domain Name System Security (DNSSEC) adds an extra layer of authenticity to responses, making it harder for spoofed records to be exploited. Some of the newer transports, like DoH and DoT, encrypt DNS queries, which changes where the resolver is placed and the filtering strategies used. For authentication and directory lookups, LDAP is used for identity attributes, and for API endpoints, RESTful URIs and URLs are used, along with input validation and rate limits. And for remote management, SSH is the go-to over older methods like PPTP. For secure mail, it's all about S/MIME for those signed and encrypted messages.

At the network layer, IPSec with AH and ESP secures site-to-site tunnels; ESP provides confidentiality while AH ensures packet integrity in specific setups. ICMP is still handy for diagnostics, but if it's exposed, it can show the topology. We still see POP in old mail stacks and it needs to be controlled carefully at the gateway. IRC is still used in some specialist operations as a chat medium, but we can't rely on it for sensitive coordination. Rather than just knowing the protocols, we need to know where to place filters, inspection points and logging so that a coherent policy can protect connections from end to end.

AH

Authentication Header

One of the best things about an Authentication Header is that it offers packet-level integrity and authentication without encrypting payloads. One thing we do is use AH in IPsec site-to-site tunnels to make sure that each IP packet's header and data stay the same when they're being sent through. So, if we have got an enterprise network, we can count on AH to keep the routing metadata safe from spoofing or replay attacks, making sure that the routing updates are always trustworthy. There are tools that check AH's cryptographic signature against shared secrets, and they flag any packets that don't match as a potential security risk. The AH parameters, integrity algorithms and sequence counters are configured in firewall policies and network device settings to enforce strict path-integrity checks across trusted links.

ESP

Encapsulated Security Payload

As for Encapsulated Security Payload, well, that encrypts IP packet payloads and can do integrity checks too, if we need them. We can set up a VPN tunnel between data centres and choose ESP to hide traffic like database replication streams from anyone trying to eavesdrop. In terms of configuration, we need to choose cipher suites. For combined encryption and authentication, go for AES-GCM, or for separate integrity, you'll need AES-CBC with HMAC, as well as tunnel or transport modes. So, we keep an eye on how well things are performing, because strong algorithms need CPU cycles, and we rotate keys regularly to keep things confidential. And network management consoles show ESP tunnel status and throughput metrics to make sure encrypted traffic flows without leaks.

DNS

Domain Name System

The Domain Name System basically translates human-friendly hostnames into IP addresses that network devices can understand. The way to do this is to set up recursive and authoritative DNS servers so that queries are resolved reliably, with caching improving response times. But attackers can exploit DNS via cache poisoning and spoofing, and redirect users to malicious sites. If we want to avoid these risks, we should implement DNSSEC and configure DNS forwarders to trusted resolvers. They'll help us spot unusual lookup patterns, spikes in NXDOMAIN responses or sudden shifts in query volumes, which could indicate reconnaissance activity.

DNSSEC

DNS Security Extensions

Rather than just using the regular DNS, the DNS Security Extensions add an extra layer of cryptographic validation, which stops spoofed or tampered responses. When we enable DNSSEC, each signed DNS record carries an RRSIG signature that resolvers check against public keys in DNSKEY records. So, these chain-of-trust setups start at the root zone, then work their way down through the TLD and authoritative zones. And we generate and roll over keys carefully to avoid resolution failures, updating DS records at the registrar. If there are any issues with the signature expiring or being validated, you'll get an automated alert, so we can be sure that the name resolution is always going to be authenticated and uninterrupted. Basically, DNSSEC turns DNS into a verified, integrity-checked system, so it's not just something we can trust on first use.

TCP/IP

Transmission Control Protocol/Internet Protocol

A TCP/IP suite is key to making sure the communications are reliable and focused on connections. Your job is to look at the three-way handshake (TCP's SYN, SYN-ACK and ACK) to figure out what's gone wrong with the session setups and tweak the congestion-control parameters for high-latency links. There are different ways of setting up IP addressing schemes, like IPv4 or IPv6, and these decide how the subnet design and routing table entries are organised. So, TCP/IP security is all about setting up firewall rules to control port access, having intrusion-prevention systems that inspect packet payloads, and using network segmentation with ACLs.

UDP

User Datagram Protocol

A User Datagram Protocol is great for low-overhead, connectionless communication. These days, services like DNS queries, voice-over-IP and streaming media are all about speed, not about making sure things get delivered. All we need to do is configure rate-limiting and ACL rules to stop UDP-based amplification attacks, DNS or NTP reflection, which can overwhelm targets. But keeping an eye on flow records lets us spot sudden spikes in UDP traffic, which might mean scanning or exfiltration attempts. There's no built-in retransmission or ordering in UDP, but application-layer protocols often implement their own checks. If we get how UDP fits into the architecture, we can make sure we have got the right safeguards in place for performance-sensitive and security-critical use cases.

HTTP

Hypertext Transfer Protocol

A Hypertext Transfer Protocol is basically a set of rules that tells clients how to ask web servers for stuff like HTML, images or API endpoints. The plan is to study HTTP methods (GET, POST, PUT, DELETE) so we can create secure request-handling logic that validates inputs and mitigates injection threats. There are a few other things we can do to help, like Response headers, Content-Security-Policy and X-Frame-Options, which help stop cross-site scripting and clickjacking. The load balancers and web servers generate access logs that go into SIEM systems, which lets us spot unusual user-agent strings or SQL-injection patterns. Almost every web application uses HTTP, so it's important to understand how it works and the security headers.

HTTPS

HTTP Secure

With an HTTPS configuration, HTTP traffic is wrapped within a TLS tunnel, which ensures confidentiality and integrity. It's all about getting those certificates from public or private CAs, slapping them on web servers, and making sure those HSTS policies are in place to stop those pesky downgrade attacks. The reverse-proxy appliances and API gateways often terminate TLS, so the cryptographic workloads don't have to be done by the backend servers. If we keep an eye on when certificates are about to expire and make sure the ciphers are up to scratch, we can make sure HTTPS deployments stay strong and follow the security standards.

ICMP

Internet Control Message Protocol

An Internet Control Message Protocol supports network diagnostics and error reporting. The team uses ICMP echo requests (ping) to check if they can reach things, and traceroute operations to map out packet paths. If we see too many or the wrong kind of ICMP packets, it might mean someone's scanning or doing reconnaissance, so we might want to apply rate-limiting or ACL filters. They do this by identifying the essential ICMP types, like echo-reply and destination-unreachable, and blocking the unnecessary ones to reduce the attack surface. It'll flag up any ICMP anomalies, helping us to tell the difference between good diagnostics and potential probing by bad guys.

IPSec

Internet Protocol Security

It's a suite of Internet Protocol Security tools that secures network-layer communications using AH and ESP, with IKE handling key exchanges. We use IPSec tunnels to connect branch offices over the Internet or to create secure microsegment boundaries within data centres. The policy definitions include stuff on encryption and integrity algorithms, lifetimes and tunnel selectors. And NAC integrations make sure that only endpoints that are compliant establish IPSec connections. We can troubleshoot by checking Security Parameter Indexes (SPI) and packet counters to verify SA negotiations. And because it's so versatile, it's a key part of creating secure layers on top of networks we can't trust.

IRC

Internet Relay Chat

IRC is a protocol that allows us to chat with other people in real-time, either in channels or private messages. People who are after us sometimes use IRC networks for command-and-control channels because they're simple and quick. When we are auditing IRC usage in the organisation, we use secure tunnels, SSH or VPN to protect channel traffic and monitor for suspicious bot activity. It's a good idea to log chat transcripts and apply keyword filters, as this can help us detect data exfiltration or insider threats. Although it's mostly been replaced by modern collaboration platforms, IRC is still useful in some DevOps and security research situations.

LDAP

Lightweight Directory Access Protocol

A Lightweight Directory Access Protocol is a tree-structured database for identities, groups and policy attributes. The app checks that we are who we say we are and gets the OK details from LDAP, making it easy to log in. To keep the credentials safe when we are moving them around, we can use StartTLS or LDAPS to secure LDAP. And ACLs on directory entries control who can read or modify specific attributes, such as group memberships. So, backup and replication strategies make sure directory services are always available.

POP

Post Office Protocol

There's a Post Office Protocol that tells email clients how to download messages from mail servers. So, when it comes to security, it's best to use POP3S, POP over SSL/TLS, to encrypt credentials and message content when we are retrieving them. What we do is configure server-side policies to retain or delete messages after download, so we don't end up with mailbox overflow. If we keep an eye on authentication attempts and mailbox quotas, we can spot brute-force attacks and account-sharing abuses. Even though IMAP has more advanced sync features, POP is still used for simple, low-resource email access.

PPTP

Point-to-Point Tunneling Protocol

A Point-to-Point Tunnelling Protocol basically wraps PPP frames in GRE packets to establish VPN connections. Old Windows computers often have PPTP built in, but there are known problems with MS-CHAPv2 authentication, so it's not secure. The plan is to replace PPTP with L2TP/IPsec or OpenVPN, so we can phase out weak tunnels. Firewall rules can detect and block GRE-based traffic, or enforce stronger VPN protocols. If we understand the flaws in the way PPTP is designed, we can safely switch off outdated VPN services without disrupting remote-access capabilities.

SSH

Secure Shell

SSH is a Secure Shell protocol that provides encrypted command-line access and secure file transfers over TCP. Instead of passwords, public-key authentication stores authorized keys in **`~/.ssh/authorized_keys`**. Here, we make sure we have key rotation policies and disable legacy ciphers to strengthen SSH servers. It's a bit like a central hub for access, keeping track of all sessions to make sure everything's above board. And port-knocking or jump-server designs add layers of defence. The fact that it can do tunnelling, X11 sessions and port forwarding makes it perfect for secure remote administration.

S/MIME

Secure/Multipurpose Internet Mail Extensions

The Secure/Multipurpose Internet Mail Extensions standard is a way of adding encryption and digital signatures to emails using X.509 certificates. The plan is to deploy enterprise CAs and RAs to issue user certificates, and to configure mail clients to sign and encrypt based on recipient keys. S/MIME enforcement at the gateway level stops unsigned or unencrypted messages with sensitive attachments. We can be sure that everything is real and the information is protected when we use this. If we use regular certificate revocation lists or OCSP responders, revoked certificates won't be able to decrypt new mail.

URI

Uniform Resource Identifier

A Uniform Resource Identifier, or URI, is basically a way to identify resources on networks, like **`http`**, **`ftp`** or **`ldap`**. Application developers use URIs to route requests, validate parameters and prevent injection attacks. These APIs make sure that traffic is routed based on URI patterns, and they'll redirect or block requests based on the path patterns they follow. We can reduce the attack surface by creating whitelists of allowed URI prefixes. If we get URI syntax and encoding rules, we can defend against path traversal and open-redirect vulnerabilities.

URL

Uniform Resource Locator

Just so we know, a Uniform Resource Locator specifies the exact location of a resource, combining a scheme (**`https://`**), domain name, optional port and path. A web server basically maps URLs to content files or application endpoints. Their security tools check URL structures and clean up query parameters to stop cross-site scripting and open-redirect exploits. The WAF rules match URL patterns to apply rate-limiting or authentication checks before backend processing. If we are good with URLs, we can make sure that only the legit requests reach the important services.

Knowledge Check

1. Which two protocols provide integrity and optional encryption at the IP packet level?

A. DNS + DNSSEC
B. AH + ESP
C. HTTP + HTTPS
D. URI + URL

2. Which pair secures web traffic and ensures confidentiality and integrity for HTTP exchanges?

A. HTTP + SSH
B. HTTPS + S/MIME
C. HTTP + POP
D. HTTP + HTTPS

3. Which two work together to validate DNS responses against tampering?

A. DNS + DNSSEC
B. DNSSEC + ICMP
C. API + URI
D. DNS + UDP

4. Which combination represents the core transport layer protocols of the Internet?
   A. TCP/IP + UDP
   B. IPSec + PPTP
   C. SSH + IRC
   D. API + URL

5. Which two enable secure remote shell access and encrypted site-to-site tunnels?
   A. SSH + IPSec
   B. SSH + UDP
   C. POP + PPTP
   D. ICMP + DNSSEC

6. Which pair would we choose for setting up a legacy VPN and a modern, stronger VPN?
   A. PPTP + IPSec
   B. PPTP + DNS
   C. ESP + HTTP
   D. LDAP + API

7. Which two protocols facilitate directory lookups and real-time text chat?
   A. LDAP + IRC
   B. LDAP + DNSSEC
   C. IRC + POP
   D. API + URL

8. Which combination handles simple mail retrieval and secure message signing?
   A. POP + S/MIME
   B. HTTP + SSH
   C. POP + IRC
   D. DNS + ICMP

9. Which two acronyms identify and locate resources on the web and APIs?
   A. URI + URL
   B. API + PPTP
   C. TCP/IP + UDP
   D. DNSSEC + ESP

10. Which pair provides network diagnostics and error reporting?
   A. ICMP + UDP
   B. ICMP + DNS
   C. ICMP + HTTP
   D. ICMP + SSL

Answer Key:

1. B
2. D
3. A
4. A
5. A
6. A
7. A
8. A
9. A
10. A

Policies, Standards & Frameworks

What we're trying to do is make policy more understandable so that controls actually work where they're needed. First, we need to do an BIA to see which systems break the business when they fail. Then, we can use that info to set RTO and RPO inside the BCP. A good BCP gets plans into action during outages, not just leaving them as hopes.

When it comes to cryptographic trust, a CA issues certificates while a CP records the steps to recover when a key is lost or a signing authority is compromised. The EULA and FACL are basically the rules for how software and file permissions work in practice, and they're the go-to docs when we're looking into misuse. So, technical controls like FDE make sure the rules are followed at the device level, which keeps the data protected even if the hardware gets lost. So, a GRC approach ties together risk, controls and audit evidence, so that compliance work isn't just in spreadsheets.

The GDPR and HIPAA set out the rules for how personal and health data has to be handled, so any operational decisions, like logging, retention and consent flows, have to reflect those laws. ISO and NIST provide a shared language for controls and assessments, while PCI DSS and SOX set out industry-specific rules that affect things like architecture, logging and change control. Keep evidence organised, test the plans on a schedule, and map each technical control back to the policy it implements so that auditors, operators and stakeholders see the same reality.

BCP

Business Continuity Planning

This is important because if a business's IT systems fail, for example if there's a ransomware attack or a natural disaster, a business continuity plan makes sure the business can keep running. For example, we can identify essential services like customer support or order processing and set targets for how long they should take. They're like pretend exercises where they act out different scenarios to show where there are communication gaps or not enough resources. Those in charge of risk management and the execs will review the plan to get insurance and keep stakeholders happy. They're updated regularly to keep up with changes in infrastructure or business priorities, so the BCP stays effective when things go wrong. It's there to help keep things running smoothly in times of crisis.

BIA

Business Impact Analysis

There's a way of working out how outages affect a business, and that's called a business impact analysis. It shows how things like service outages can impact revenue, operations and reputation. As part of this, you'll be interviewing department leads to map out critical applications, data feeds and third-party dependencies. The findings help to set recovery point objectives, and define acceptable data-loss windows for each function. They also highlight "firewall" processes, which are the ones most likely to fail and cause the most harm. At the board level, they translate technical risks into financial terms, guiding investments in redundancy or cloud failover. And we do annual reviews to make sure the BIA adapts to new products, changes in the regulatory landscape or shifts in the market. It's all about making sure continuity planning stays in sync with the evolving needs of the business.

CA

Certificate Authority

Every secure website or email system relies on a trusted certificate authority to link public keys to verified identities. The first thing we need to do is set up a hierarchical PKI, which involves keeping the root CA keys safe and sound inside hardware security modules. We then need to delegate issuance to subordinate CAs. These guys make sure that everything is legit by doing identity checks, document validation, and out-of-band approvals before signing certificates. There are policy definitions on key lengths, validity periods and approved algorithms that help to keep cryptographic trust.

CP

Contingency Planning

What happens when things go wrong? I'm talking about system failures, data corruption or security breaches. A contingency plan is a set of instructions for how to deal with these issues. So, you'll be working with the IT, facilities and communications teams to document things like failover procedures, notification templates and escalation paths. The playbooks are there to help teams activate backup data centres, restore critical backups and update stakeholders. After the event, reviews look at what went well and what didn't, and use this to make improvements to plans for if things go wrong and for things that should be done regularly. It's all about making sure that the legal, operational and public relations sides are all on the same page, so that we can get back on track quickly and efficiently if something goes wrong.

EULA

End User License Agreement

Just so we know, any third-party software we install has its own end user licence agreement that sets out how it can be used. The legal team will help us write EULA clauses that say the software can't be reverse engineered, redistributed or modified without permission. When we install something, we have got to accept a EULA, and that creates a record of consent. The software-asset management team uses the EULA terms when they're doing audits, and this helps them to spot any unlicensed or unsupported apps that could create problems. It's important to have clear and enforceable EULAs in place. They help us to mitigate legal risk, manage vendor relationships and maintain a secure, compliant software estate across the enterprise.

FACL

File Access Control List

The file access control lists tell us who can read, write or execute each file. It's all about setting up ACL entries for user groups and roles, making sure only the right people can get into financial records or HR documents. Then there are automated tools that compare the actual FACL settings against policy baselines, flagging any permissions that are too high and putting measures in place to fix them. When we're investigating something, our incident responders will have a look at the change logs to see if there's any unauthorised modifications. And when we manage the access control lists (ACLs) consistently, it means we are following the principle of least privilege at the file system level. This makes reporting compliance much easier, as we have got a clear overview of who has access to what.

FDE

Full-Disk Encryption

We all know how important it is to keep data safe, right? Well, the first step is to encrypt the whole disk, which protects every sector on a storage device. It's a piece of cake to install FDE agents on the laptops, desktops and removable drives, and it works with TPM modules to keep the encryption keys safe and sound. As we know, pre-boot authentication requires users to enter credentials or insert smart cards before the operating system loads. The idea is that we store the recovery keys on a central server so that, if we forget the password, we can still access the data. It'll do a compliance audit to check the encryption status of all the devices we are managing, and a health check to see if there are any disks that aren't encrypted or are set up wrong.

GRC

Governance, Risk & Compliance

In situations where we need to see the bigger picture when it comes to policies, risks and controls, a GRC platform is the place to go. It's all about importing regulatory frameworks like ISO 27001, NIST CSF, and PCI DSS, and then mapping each control to the technical set-up, documentation, and incident logs. The automated workflows do things like risk assessments, assigning remediation tickets and producing executive summaries. The dashboards show compliance scores and risk heat maps to help with planning. It integrates with SIEM and CSPM tools so that any policy violations that are detected automatically enter the GRC workflow, closing the loop between monitoring and enforcement. With GRC, we can bring together all the different compliance tasks and make them into one process that's all about risk.

GDPR

General Data Protection Regulation

Every organisation dealing with the personal data of EU citizens must comply with the general data protection regulation. First, we map data flows to identify personally identifiable information, then we implement consent-management systems that let individuals grant or revoke permissions. Basically, data protection impact assessments look at new processing activities and guide decisions on things like pseudonymisation or encryption. The rules say we have got to let the right people know within a week. We can use data subject access request workflows to view, correct or delete the records. And with GDPR's big fines, which can hit up to 4% of global turnover, it's more important than ever to have solid data governance and build trust with customers.

HIPAA

Health Insurance Portability and Accountability Act

The HIPAA technical and administrative safeguards are there to help healthcare providers protect electronic protected health information. It's all about making sure that only the right people can access the clinical systems, and that everyone has the right permissions. The audit logs keep track of who accesses and modifies what, which is useful for investigating breaches. And if we want to keep the ePHI safe in transit and at rest, we can rest assured that it meets HIPAA's requirements for secure data handling. As part of this, you'll be setting up business associate agreements with vendors, which will extend HIPAA controls beyond the walls. And we do regular risk analyses and staff training, so everyone knows what they're responsible for.

ISO

International Organization for Standardization

The International Organization for Standardization has codified best practices for information security, privacy and continuity management. It's a way of setting up an Information Security Management System, following Plan-Do-Check-Act cycles for ongoing improvement. And on top of that, certification audits make sure the ISMS is up to scratch and show customers and partners how good it is. There are some extra standards that go along with the main ones, like ISO 22301 for business continuity and ISO 27701 for managing personal data. These standards make sure that governance is applied to related areas too. But if we make sure we include the ISO requirements in policy documents and GRC systems, we can make sure the controls stay consistent across the global operations.

NIST

National Institute of Standards and Technology

The National Institute of Standards and Technology (NIST) gives us the lowdown on how to follow federal and industry best practices. For example, we can use the NIST Cybersecurity Framework's five functions to structure program activities. These are Identify, Protect, Detect, Respond and Recover. There are some great resources out there, like SP800-53 for control baselines and SP800-171 for controlled unclassified information, which can help inform selection and configuration of technical safeguards. And the Risk Management Framework makes sure security is part of the system development lifecycle. So, when we map NIST controls to ISO 27001 or regulatory requirements within a GRC platform, it makes sure everything's in line with the rules, and we've got clear audit trails. That way, we can be sure our security is solid and we can prove it too.

PCI DSS

Payment Card Industry Data Security Standard

All the companies and people who deal with cardholder data follow PCI DSS to keep payment transactions safe. It separates payment systems from the general networks and makes sure that only authorised people can access the systems that process, store or transmit card data. Our encryption requirements cover data in transit and at rest, and we do quarterly vulnerability scans and annual penetration tests to make sure our defences are up to scratch. So, in the event of a breach, the incident-response playbooks include steps for getting ready to handle the investigation. There are different assessment requirements for each merchant tier, from self-assessment questionnaires to audits by qualified security assessors. But to avoid fines and keep people's trust in the brand, every payment company must comply.

SOX

Sarbanes-Oxley Act

The Sarbanes-Oxley Act is there to make sure public companies are being honest about their financial reports. It's all about implementing IT general controls, change management, access reviews and audit logging on financial systems to stop unauthorised modifications. Then there's Section 404, which makes management and external auditors promise that internal controls over financial reporting are working. All these systems pull together evidence, policies, procedures and log data to make attestations easier.

Knowledge Check

1. Which two prepare organizations to continue critical operations during and after disruptive events?

A. EULA + FACL
B. CA + CP
C. BCP + BIA
D. PCI DSS + SOX

2. Which pair binds cryptographic trust and outlines immediate response steps for crises?

A. GDPR + HIPAA
B. CA + CP
C. ISO + NIST
D. FDE + GRC

3. Which two govern permitted software usage and file-system permissions?

A. BCP + BIA
B. ISO + SOX
C. PCI DSS + HIPAA
D. EULA + FACL

4. Which combination enforces full-disk encryption and integrates policy, risk and compliance workflows?

A. FDE + GRC
B. CA + CP
C. ISO + NIST
D. BIA + EULA

5. Which duo establishes legal requirements for protecting EU personal data and US health information?

A. PCI DSS + SOX
B. ISO + SOX
C. GDPR + HIPAA
D. FACL + EULA

6. Which two provide international best-practice frameworks and detailed control guidance?
A. BCP + CP
B. ISO + NIST
C. GRC + FDE
D. GDPR + PCI DSS

7. Which pair applies specifically to payment-card security and financial-reporting integrity?
A. HIPAA + GDPR
B. CA + CP
C. ISO + NIST
D. PCI DSS + SOX

8. Which combination addresses both immediate contingency actions and overall continuity planning?
A. CP + BCP
B. FACL + EULA
C. PCI DSS + GRC
D. ISO + HIPAA

9. Which two involve external certification audits and attestations to demonstrate control effectiveness?
A. EULA + CP
B. ISO + SOX
C. GDPR + HIPAA
D. BIA + BCP

10. Which duo maps technical controls to regulatory requirements and automates compliance tracking?
A. FDE + CA
B. EULA + FACL
C. GRC + NIST
D. PCI DSS + BIA

Answer Key:

1. C

2. B

3. D
4. A
5. C
6. B
7. D
8. A
9. B
10. C

Physical & Environmental Controls

Physical and environmental controls protect the infrastructure that runs services and the data those services hold. The first line is access control at the site level: badge readers, mantraps and door strikes restrict who can reach server rooms and cages. A visitor log and escorted access procedures provide accountability while rack locking and secure cages limit hands-on access to hardware. CCTV coverage complements access controls by recording movement and providing forensic footage when incidents require reconstruction.

Power and cooling form the next layer of defense. UPS systems keep critical gear online through short outages and provide graceful shutdown signals when needed. PDU monitoring traces load and power distribution so overloads or failures surface before systems degrade. HVAC units regulate temperature and humidity to prevent hardware faults; environmental sensors detect water, smoke, or temperature excursions and feed alerts into the operations pipeline. Redundancy planning such as N+1 power and dual-feed HVAC helps maintain availability during component failures.

Integration matters as much as devices. Syslog, SIEM and facility management platforms ingest alarms from CCTV, UPS, PDUs and sensors so operators see a unified incident picture. Regular testing of failover procedures, battery replacements and CCTV retention policies preserves evidence integrity and minimizes surprises during audits. A coordinated change process ties physical work orders to security approvals so maintenance actions do not create unintended exposures. With these controls aligned, the facility becomes a resilient platform that supports secure operation and reliable incident response.

CCTV

Closed-Circuit Television

A closed-circuit television system lets us observe physical spaces in real time and review recorded footage when incidents occur. The security teams do install CCTV cameras at data-center entrances, server racks and network closets such that they can deter the unauthorized access and capture detailed video evidence. Its intelligent analytics flag the unusual behaviors, tailgating or access-card misuse, and send alerts to the security operations center the moment they find suspicion. We need to treat the CCTV as the organization's digital eyewitness as it provides the visual context for security investigations and helps in verifying that physical controls and access policies are enforced consistently around the clock.

HVAC

Heating, Ventilation and Air-Conditioning

As we all know, a heating, ventilation and air-conditioning system is vital for keeping the temperature and humidity levels right for the hardware to work properly. The idea is to set the HVAC units to keep the server rooms at between 18 and 27 degrees Celsius, with the humidity at around 40 to 60 per cent. If the temperature gets too high or there's not enough airflow, environmental sensors will send us an alert. Then we can check if there's a problem with the cooling or something's blocking the airflow. Things like regular maintenance, replacing filters and cleaning coils can help stop the engine overheating. The HVAC system is like the heartbeat of the physical infrastructure. If the environment is consistent, it keeps the servers from overheating and breaking, which could lead to downtime or data loss.

PDU

Power Distribution Unit

Basically, a power distribution unit is a device that can supply electricity to a number of devices in a rack or cabinet. It usually has circuit-level monitoring and remote switch capabilities. They're used to balance loads, prevent overloads and track power consumption at the outlet level. With networked PDUs, we can get info on voltage, current and power-factor straight to the infrastructure management system, which makes it easy to spot hotspots or equipment that's not being used to its full potential. And remote outlet control lets us power-cycle hung servers without having to send technicians out to the site.

UPS

Uninterruptible Power Supply

This is an uninterruptible power supply, which gives us short-term battery backup when the power goes off or gets really unstable. The idea is to hook up important devices, servers, network switches and storage arrays to a UPS so we can keep going even when there's an outage or brownout, and make sure the data doesn't get corrupted. If the battery gets low, the automatic shutdown scripts kick in to make sure the system powers off without a hitch. If we do regular self-tests and replace the batteries, that'll keep everything running smoothly. And if we use SNMP or REST-API integrations, we can get status updates into the monitoring platforms.

Knowledge Check

1. Which two controls work together to ensure continuous video surveillance during a power outage?

A. CCTV + UPS

B. HVAC + PDU

C. PDU + UPS

D. CCTV + HVAC

2. Which pair maintains optimal data-center temperature and provides emergency backup power?

A. CCTV + PDU

B. HVAC + UPS

C. PDU + CCTV

D. HVAC + CCTV

3. Which duo offers rack-level power monitoring and automated shutdown during grid failures?

A. PDU + UPS

B. CCTV + UPS

C. HVAC + PDU

D. PDU + CCTV

4. Which two systems require testing of airflow sensors and battery capacity to validate readiness?

A. HVAC + UPS

B. CCTV + UPS

C. HVAC + CCTV

D. PDU + UPS

5. Which combination helps us detect unauthorized access visually and verify environmental breaches?

A. CCTV + HVAC

B. PDU + UPS

C. CCTV + PDU

D. HVAC + UPS

6. Which pair enables us to remotely power-cycle hung servers and track outlet-level consumption?

A. UPS + CCTV

B. PDU + UPS

C. HVAC + PDU

D. CCTV + HVAC

7. Which two controls form the backbone of data-center resilience against thermal stress and blackouts?

A. HVAC + UPS

B. CCTV + PDU

C. PDU + CCTV

D. HVAC + CCTV

8. Which duo would we include in a drill that simulates loss of mains power and reviews camera failover?

A. UPS + CCTV

B. HVAC + PDU

C. UPS + HVAC

D. PDU + CCTV

9. Which pair integrates with the infrastructure dashboard to show temperature metrics and power draw?

A. CCTV + HVAC

B. HVAC + PDU

C. PDU + UPS

D. CCTV + UPS

10. Which two require regular preventive maintenance such as filter changes and battery replacements?

A. HVAC + UPS

B. CCTV + PDU

C. HVAC + CCTV

D. PDU + UPS

Answer Key:

1. A

2. B

3. A

4. A

5. A

6. B

7. A

8. A

9. B

10. A

Part II: Threats, Vulnerabilities & Mitigations

Threat Actors & Motivations

Having an understanding of who is targeting the systems and why they are doing so is necessary for preventing attacks. For this analysis, we will examine a variety of adversaries, ranging from slow, state-sponsored campaigns to swift, opportunistic blows.

The two most common kinds of cyber attacks are known as Advanced Persistent Threats (APT) and Denial-of-Service attacks (DoS, DDoS). The first type is quite sophisticated and difficult to detect, whereas the second type is more concerned with bringing the system to its knees by sending a great deal of traffic in the opposite direction. There are a few different ways in which Open-Source Intelligence (OSINT) and Enterprise Social Networking (ESN) platforms can be of assistance. It is possible to use them for both working together and conducting reconnaissance. In addition, vulnerabilities such as Remote Access Trojans (RAT) and Remote Code Execution (RCE) are comparable to security backdoors.

Furthermore, there are exploits known as Remote File Inclusion (RFI) and Return-Oriented Programming (ROP), which are essentially exploits that take advantage of code that is already present. In addition, there is a technique known as Cross-Site Scripting (XSS), which disrupts the browser of the user. Also, the ATT&CK framework that MITRE has developed is an excellent tool for monitoring all these risk metrics and tactics. In addition, we can assign a monetary value to potential dangers by utilizing metrics such as Annualized Loss Expectancy (ALE) and Annual Rate of Occurrence (ARO).

APT

Advanced Persistent Threat

Can we imagine a sneaky hacker living undetected in the network for months, gathering sensitive data one byte at a time? The state-sponsored groups often use spear-phishing to get into a system first, then install custom malware and disable logs. It'd be the job to hunt for irregular service account logins at odd hours, track encrypted outbound channels and monitor for unauthorised lateral movement. And with real-time endpoint telemetry paired with threat-intelligence indicators, we can keep an eye out for those subtle footprints. We should treat an APT like a silent spy: detecting it requires patience, deep forensic analysis and proactive threat hunts rather than simple firewall rules.

DDoS

Distributed Denial of Service

If we picture thousands of hijacked devices swarming the web server with fake requests until real users can't connect, that's exactly what's going to happen. At busy times, retailers and game publishers are facing this threat, where attackers are demanding ransom payments to end the attack. Then we set up the network to send traffic through a cloud-based scrubbing service that filters out malicious packets, while the on-premises edge devices enforce rate limits per source. And if we are monitoring request rates and geolocation patterns, you'll be alerted to any unusual surges. It's like a mob trying to block the entrance to a store, and effective defences either thin out the crowd or reroute it through checkpoints.

DoS

Denial of Service

One bad machine can send so many requests to the service that it uses up all the CPU or memory, which can stop the applications. So, small-scale web servers or IoT devices are easy targets. The first thing we do is set connection rate thresholds and then inspect packet payloads for known attack signatures on the firewalls. We can also use application-level controls, like setting a maximum number of sessions, to prevent the resources from being used up. It's like one person chaining the data centre's door shut. We need ways to quickly spot and remove that troublemaker before the whole service locks down.

ESN

Enterprise Social Networking

The organization's internal chat and collaboration platform accelerates teamwork but can also leak data when misconfigured, such as let us say that a confidential design document shared in a private channel that an integration bot inadvertently posts to an external repository. So here, we enforce data-loss prevention policies on the ESN, blocking sensitive file types and scanning messages for proprietary keywords. We audit the logs that were tracking the file-sharing events and unusual downloads. The ESN is generally treated as a corporate watercooler, which is valuable for discussion yet requiring moderation, oversight and technical guardrails to keep sensitive information from wandering beyond approved groups.

OSINT

Open-Source Intelligence

A team often notices that public traces reveal more than expected. When we scan the pastebin dumps, or browsing the job posts with stray internal emails or when we look at certificate records listing forgotten domains, we generally notice that how the OSINT becomes a quiet mirror. It feels similar to checking what an outsider would see if they looked at the organization through public lenses. As we place these findings next to ongoing assessments, forgotten patches and overlooked endpoints start surfacing. The OSINT works like holding a torch over publicly available clues so exposed edges can be fixed before someone with bad intentions notices them.

RAT

Remote Access Trojan

An unwanted foothold usually begins when a malicious file blends into a normal workflow and installs a hidden controller inside an endpoint. When the device starts reaching out on unusual ports, the monitoring tools raise the first signs of trouble. The network rules shut down the suspicious channels, and containment removes the infected device from the main environment. As processes are reviewed, the odd child tasks linked to browsers or file viewers draw attention. The RAT feels like an invisible door. It is added to the machine without permission, and it is quietly copying keystrokes and movements.

RCE

Remote Code Execution

A small slip inside an application can feel like leaving a door slightly open, giving someone a chance to run commands on the server without being noticed. Now here, generally the monitoring tools usually spot this early when they catch strange requests that look a bit like shell instructions sneaking through. However here, the quick patching and tighter filters help close that opening before anything harmful settles in. While sorting things out, the affected server is kept aside and fresh keys are placed so nothing unwanted remains. In all, the RCE feels like letting someone else tap away on the keyboard, which is why simple input checks and low-access permissions go a long way in keeping the control with us.

RFI

Remote File Inclusion

If we allow file paths from places we don't trust, the system can end up grabbing and running files that we didn't intend to use. The scanner quickly points out **`include`** or **`require`** statements that reach out to remote sources. If we keep file paths limited to safe folders and switch off remote wrappers, the application won't pull in outside scripts. At RFI, it's a bit like letting someone turn up to a movie night with their own disc without checking what's on it. It's just a matter of simple checks and firm server settings, and the app won't load anything it shouldn't.

ROP

Return-Oriented Programming

Nowadays, there are ways of stopping injected code, but ROP attackers can chain together tiny bits of existing code and gadgets to perform arbitrary operations. The hardened binaries disrupt typical gadget sequences through address space layout randomisation, while control-flow integrity features detect unusual return-address jumps. When we're investigating incidents, we look for patterns in how gadgets are run in memory-dump analysis. It's like ROP is putting together a new tool from bits of old factory parts; only a strong "lockdown" of memory and strict executable permissions stop attackers from putting those dangerous gadgets back together again.

XSS

Cross-Site Scripting

When web pages don't encode user inputs, it's a problem. Because attackers can inject scripts that run in other users' browsers. This can result in cookies being stolen or users being redirected to malicious sites. As part of this, we use templating frameworks that automatically escape output, enforce strict content security policies and scan for common payload patterns during code reviews. We can test with real-world payloads, like script tags, to confirm the defences. To put it simply, XSS is like graffiti on storefront windows, tricking people into unsafe behaviour. But don't worry, thorough sanitisation and browser hardening keep the site walls clean.

ATT&CK

Adversarial Tactics, Techniques and Common Knowledge

These days, security pros use a framework called ATT&CK to map observed behaviours, like credential dumping or command-and-control protocols, to a standardised taxonomy. The idea is to build detection rules in the SIEM that are aligned with ATT&CK technique IDs, so we can have consistent incident-response playbooks. The threat-intelligence feeds use ATT&CK to clearly describe the campaigns of the bad guys. They're like training exercises, but for real-life scenarios. They map these scenarios to specific ATT&CK techniques, so the team gets to practise identifying and fixing problems.

ALE

Annualized Loss Expectancy

The best way to show that we are worth the money is to calculate the expected loss over the year. The way to do it is to work out how much we think you'll lose, how much it'll cost you, and then multiply that by how often we think ransomware attacks happen in a year. That'll give us an idea of how much you'll lose each year. This metric helps decision-makers when they're talking about budgets, showing which DDoS mitigation service or extended backups will get better value for money. If we can picture it, ALE is like a crystal ball for the security budget, helping us to see what's coming up so we can make the best use of the resources and reduce risk.

ARO

Annual Rate of Occurrence

The more we can work out how often a threat is likely to happen each year, the better we can judge the risks. It's all about looking at past incidents, like how often people fell for phishing attempts or how often hardware broke, to figure out ARO values. If we pair ARO with single loss expectancy, we can work out the ALE, which helps us to put together a data-driven risk treatment plan. We can think of ARO as the event calendar that shows when we expect an attack or failure to happen. If we can predict these things accurately, we can make sure we focus our defences on the threats most likely to strike within the planning horizon.

Knowledge Check

1. When a campaign remains hidden for months, exfiltrating data in small increments, we are most likely facing which threat?
    A. DDoS
    B. APT
    C. XSS
    D. RFI

2. A sudden flood of HTTP requests from thousands of IoT devices describes which attack?
    A. DoS
    B. RCE
    C. DDoS
    D. ALE

3. Which technique chains return instructions in existing code to bypass non-executable memory protections?
    A. ROP
    B. RAT
    C. RFI
    D. OSINT

4. We spot browser alerts showing <script> tags injected into comment fields. That indicates:
    A. RCE
    B. XSS
    C. ARO
    D. ESN

5. Gathering employee profiles from LinkedIn and job postings to plan an intrusion exemplifies:
    A. RAT
    B. OSINT
    C. ATT&CK
    D. FDE

6. A formula multiplying single loss expectancy by annual probability yields:
    A. ARO
    B. ALE
    C. RFI
    D. BIA

7. Which rule set helps the SOC map detected behaviors, like credential dumping, to a standardized taxonomy?
    A. ALE
    B. ATT&CK
    C. APT
    D. PDU

8. When a web app fetches a malicious PHP script specified by a user-supplied URL, we are seeing:
    A. RCE
    B. RFI
    C. DDoS
    D. XSS

9. A single-source flood of malformed ICMP packets overwhelming a device describes:
    A. DDoS
    B. DoS
    C. RAT
    D. ESN

10. We predict five phishing incidents per year based on past data. That figure represents:
    A. ARO
    B. ALE
    C. ROP
    D. CP

Answer Key:

1. B
2. C
3. A
4. B
5. B

6. B
7. B
8. B
9. B
10. A

Malware & Attack Techniques

One must first comprehend the methods by which attackers employ protocols and code as weapons to construct efficient defenses. This section will study common malware and exploitation techniques, covering everything from file-based threats to complicated web-application vulnerabilities. At the most basic level, there is antivirus software and endpoint security measures in place to prevent malicious software and legitimate automation. However, scripting languages like BASH and VBA as well as dynamic-link libraries (DLL) present opportunities for harm. Malicious software and spam emails prey on people's gullibility. Injection of SQL queries (SQLi) and cross-site request forgery (CSRF/XSRF) exploit weaknesses in online form security.

Both scripting-based remote code execution and local file inclusion (LFI) are examples of inclusion vulnerabilities that can lead to backdoors. These protocol flaws reveal possible dangers, for example, CHAP replay attacks and DEP bypasses. When it comes to response and logging, NSPs make things easier. The scanning of computers for PUPs, DEP configuration, and web form strength are just a few examples of the everyday tasks that will serve as the basis for all the terms.

AV

Antivirus

Antivirus software, when installed on endpoints, enables the systems to detect known malware families through signature-based and heuristic engines. Prior to consumers running any files from USB devices or email attachments, scanning schedules are catching them. When behavioral analysis modules detect suspicious process activity, such as Word creating unanticipated child processes, they trigger quarantine procedures. Antivirus software is like a watchdog: it keeps an eye out for recognized threats and lets us know when something fishy tries to sneak by, so we can investigate before the problem escalates.

BASH

Bourne Again Shell

When we automate tasks on Linux servers with BASH scripts, we benefit from powerful command-line utilities, but attackers exploit that same power for malicious purposes. Threat actors embed reverse shells in cron jobs or craft one-liner payloads that download and execute malware with **`curl|bash`**.

The hardening strategy includes disabling unnecessary shell access, enforcing multi-factor SSH, and restricting script execution to approved directories. Treat BASH as a double-edged sword: essential for system administration yet dangerous when scripts execute untrusted code. Proper permissions and script signing help ensure that only authorized, reviewed scripts run on the servers.

BEC

Business Email Compromise

When attackers spoof executives' email addresses or compromise accounts, they trick employees into transferring funds or sharing sensitive data. We train staff to verify unusual requests, such as changes to payment instructions, through secondary channels like phone calls. Email-security gateways apply advanced spoof-protection and anomaly detection to flag mismatches in sender domains and content patterns. Incident-response playbooks define steps for rapid account lockouts, forensic mailbox reviews and notification of finance and legal teams. Consider BEC as a con artist posing as the CEO over email; strict verification policies and technical filters serve as the scam-detecting lie-detector test.

CSRF

Cross-Site Request Forgery

When we protect web applications, CSRF defenses prevent attackers from tricking authenticated users into submitting unintended requests. The developers implement anti-CSRF tokens embedded in each form, validated on the server side to confirm legitimate origins. HTTP-only cookies and same-site attributes further reduce attack surfaces. Testing with crafted HTML pages confirms that state-changing actions, like password updates or fund transfers, resist unauthorized form submissions. Picture CSRF as a hidden instruction slipping into a trusted webpage, ordering the browser to perform actions we didn't intend; CSRF tokens act like secret handshake codes that verify genuine requests.

DLL

Dynamic-Link Library

When Windows applications load functionality at runtime, they rely on DLL files that can also serve as attack vectors. DLL hijacking occurs when an application searches for a DLL in an untrusted directory, allowing an attacker to place a malicious version that the application loads instead of the legitimate one. We enforce application-whitelisting, constrain DLL search paths and monitor filesystem changes to detect unauthorized DLL drops. Viewing DLLs as interchangeable building blocks helps us understand why proper path hardening and code-signing checks are critical to prevent attackers from slipping malicious code into the trusted libraries.

LFI

Local File Inclusion

When web applications construct file paths from user inputs without validation, they become vulnerable to LFI, permitting attackers to read sensitive server files, such as **`/etc/passwd`** or configuration files. We configure strict parameter whitelists and disable directory traversal constructs (`../`) at the web-server level. Web application firewalls inspect incoming requests for inclusion patterns and block malicious queries. Imagine LFI as an intruder insisting on reading every private memo in the office by slipping keys under the door; rigorous validation and filtering keep unauthorized paths from cracking the application's file system.

PUP

Potentially Unwanted Program

When endpoints install software that the user did not explicitly request, toolbars, ad injectors or hidden miners, antivirus flags these as PUPs. Security teams configure policies to block installations of unsigned or bundled applications and alert users when downloads include optional add-ons. Automated remediation scripts remove known PUP signatures and restore modified browser settings. Think of PUPs as "Trojan horses" carrying unwanted extras: helpful controls treat every unexpected install like potential malware until proven safe, reducing the risk of hidden surveillance or resource abuse on user machines.

SQLi

Structured Query Language Injection

When web forms embed user inputs into SQL queries without sanitization, attackers inject **`'; DROP TABLE users; --`** or other payloads that manipulate database commands. The developers use parameterized queries (prepared statements) or ORM frameworks to separate code from data. Database activity monitoring tools watch for anomalous SQL patterns and block dangerous commands. Picture SQLi as sneaking toxic instructions into the database's order sheet, forcing it to delete or expose data; parameterization and strict input validation close that loophole, ensuring that user inputs never become executable commands.

VBA

Visual Basic for Applications

When users open Office documents containing VBA macros, those macros can automate tasks, or deliver malware. Security teams disable macros by default, enabling them only for signed, verified templates. Email filters strip macro-enabled files or quarantine suspicious attachments. Sandbox analysis executes macros in isolated environments to observe malicious behaviors, such as file downloads or registry modifications, before allowing documents into production. Treat VBA macros as the scripting engine inside the document: enabling them enhances productivity but requires robust controls to prevent them from becoming malware launchers.

XSRF

Cross-Site Request Forgery

Often used interchangeably with CSRF, XSRF exploits the same vulnerability, tricking browsers into submitting forged requests on authenticated sessions. Mirroring the CSRF defenses, unique tokens, same-site cookie attributes and referer-header checks, protects against XSRF attacks. Automated test suites inject XSRF payloads to ensure that every state-changing endpoint rejects unauthorized requests. Consider XSRF as a stealth instruction embedded in a malicious webpage masquerading as the bank's portal; proper validation stops that instruction in its tracks before it executes under the credentials.

CHAP

Challenge Handshake Authentication Protocol (Replay Context)

When we secure PPP links or VPN tunnels, CHAP issues a random challenge to the client, which responds with a hashed combination of the challenge and the shared secret. Attackers capturing that handshake cannot reuse it later because each challenge is unique, preventing replay attacks. We configure CHAP on the VPN concentrators, rotating shared secrets and monitoring failed authentication attempts. Imagine CHAP as a secret quiz with a new question each session; correct answers prove identity without transmitting passwords, and wrong answers or repeated cycles signal potential eavesdropper activity.

DEP

Data Execution Prevention

When we enable data execution prevention on workstations and servers, the operating system blocks execution of code in memory regions marked as data, thwarting many buffer-overflow exploits. Attackers forced to inject malicious shellcode into unexecutable areas find their payloads unable to run. The endpoint hardening policies activate DEP across processors supporting the NX bit, and registry settings enforce always-on DEP for critical applications. Treat DEP as a fence around the executable regions: code attempting to jump over the fence into data zones triggers alarms and stops exploits in their tracks.

NSP

Network Security Platform

When we deploy a network security platform, we integrate intrusion prevention, application-level filtering and threat-intelligence feeds into a unified solution. The NSP analyzes traffic flows, inspects packet contents and applies behavioral models to detect malware, exploits and command-and-control communications. Security operations use NSP dashboards to manage alerts, quarantine affected segments and tune policies. Picture the NSP as a virtual fortress gate that not only inspects incoming visitors but also keeps an eye on unusual behaviors inside the walls, coordinating response actions across the entire network.

Knowledge Check

1. A user reports unexpected toolbar installations and browser redirects on multiple workstations. Which term describes these applications?

A. AV
B. PUP
C. DEP
D. NSP

2. An attacker crafts a URL to submit a hidden funds-transfer request while a victim is logged in. Which two controls prevent this?

A. CSRF tokens + Same-Site cookies
B. BASH scripts + VBA macros
C. CHAP + DEP
D. DLL signing + NSP

3. Which technique uses unvalidated form inputs to manipulate database queries?

A. SQLi
B. ROP
C. LFI
D. XSRF

4. The Linux server runs a curl | bash command from an unknown source. Which vector does this represent?

A. AV
B. BASH

C. VBA
D. PUP

5. An email appears to come from the CFO asking for an urgent wire transfer. Which attack method is most likely in play?
   A. BEC
   B. RCE
   C. DEP
   D. ESN

6. Which vulnerability allows attackers to read the /etc/passwd file by manipulating URL parameters?
   A. LFI
   B. SQLi
   C. XSS
   D. CHAP

7. An exploit chains small snippets of existing code to bypass non-execute memory protections. Which technique is that?
   A. ROP
   B. DEP
   C. NSP
   D. DLL

8. A user opens a downloaded document, and macros execute that install malware. Which technology did the attacker leverage?
   A. VBA
   B. BASH
   C. CSRF
   D. PUP

9. The VPN logs show repeated CHAP challenge failures followed by successful logins with old credentials. What risk does this reveal?
   A. Replay attack
   B. DDoS
   C. LFI
   D. DEP

10. Which platform inspects traffic flows, applies threat-intelligence feeds and coordinates automated responses across the network?
   A. NSP
   B. AV

C. SQLi
D. XSRF

Answer Key:

1. B
2. A
3. A
4. B
5. A
6. A
7. A
8. A
9. A
10. A

Vulnerability Assessment & Scoring

A proactive security posture depends on identifying weaknesses before attackers exploit them and prioritizing fixes based on business impact. In this subtopic, we will go into the methods for tracking vulnerabilities through CVE, assessing their severity with CVSS, and comprehending common patterns of flaws through CWE.

In contrast to machine-readable checks like OVAL, which automate assessments, public repositories like NVD store details about vulnerabilities. Given the hazards associated with control systems, the relevant industry standards are IEC 62443-3. The channels for threat intelligence (MISP, TIP, CTI) and indicators of compromise (IOC, YARA rules) augment the situation. Using metrics for risk management, ODR, NACRM, and orchestration through SOAR, we can distribute resources effectively. We can all benefit from standardized vulnerability information sharing and action thanks to frameworks like STIX2. We will learn how each acronym drives effective remediation strategies through practical exercises that involve scanning the network, interpreting scores, and integrating feeds.

CVE

Common Vulnerabilities and Exposures

When it comes to publicly known security vulnerabilities, we use the CVE catalog as our bible. Like "CVE-2024-12345: buffer overflow in XYZ library," each CVE entry gives a distinct identifier and brief description, letting us refer to and convey issues clearly. We can pinpoint which software versions need patching or compensating controls to implement when the vulnerability scanner generates a CVE-ID. The automated ticket creation for newly discovered CVEs impacting the environment is made possible through integrations with threat feeds. To better understand vendor bulletins and researcher reports, think of CVE as the security dictionary that creates a common language that everyone on the team can use.

CVSS

Common Vulnerability Scoring System

We use CVSS scores to figure out which flaws need urgent attention when we're reviewing vulnerability scan results. It considers base metrics, attack vector, complexity, privileges, as well as temporal and environmental factors, and generates a numerical score from 0.0 to 10.0. We compare scores across CVEs to decide which patches are a priority: a CVSS 9.8 critical remote-code-execution vulnerability is better than a score of 4.3 moderate information-disclosure issue. If you customise environmental metrics, you can make sure that vulnerabilities in critical infrastructure are addressed as a priority.

CWE

Common Weakness Enumeration

Whenever we're trying to work out what's causing software problems, the CWE entries help us to spot patterns like "CWE-79: Improper Neutralization of Input During Web Page Generation (Cross-Site Scripting)." What we do is map CVEs to CWEs to spot recurring weakness types in the codebase. The development teams use CWE lists to help guide secure-coding training and embed static analysis checks for high-risk categories. When we're doing code reviews, we make sure we fix the most serious CWEs before we start working on feature enhancements. It's basically a way of categorising common design and implementation errors, so we can move away from just fixing problems after they've happened and start fixing the main, most dangerous weak spots right from the start.

NVD

National Vulnerability Database

We use the National Vulnerability Database when we need detailed vulnerability information. It adds CVSS scores, impact metrics, configuration checks and references to CVE entries. Automated tools pull NVD JSON feeds to update the vulnerability management platform daily. We use NVD to filter flaws by when they were published, which products they affect and how severe they are. It's all linked to the asset inventory, so we can see which hosts or applications need urgent patching, based on the NVD data. Just think of NVD as a CVE library with loads of extra info, to help us make smart decisions about how to fix problems, instead of rushing into fixing every new flaw that comes up.

OVAL

Open Vulnerability and Assessment Language

The great thing about OVAL is that it provides a standardised XML schema for representing security content, definitions, tests, states and results. This is useful when we automate vulnerability checks across diverse systems. We import OVAL definitions for the operating systems and applications into the assessment tools, which run checks and report pass/fail outcomes. With custom OVAL content, we can check that the configuration is correct, like making sure SSH root login is disabled, without having to write any scripts by hand. So, OVAL is a kind of testing protocol that translates the security requirements into instructions that the machines can read, which means we can do consistent checks across thousands of endpoints with hardly any custom development.

IEC 62443

Industrial Automation and Control Systems Security

In the world of OT environments, power plants and manufacturing lines, IEC 62443 is the go-to standard. It covers everything from system lifecycle management to risk assessment and component security. We do zone and conduit analyses, apply security levels SL1 through SL4 to network segments, and make sure that embedded controllers meet secure-development requirements. When they're checking that the control system architecture separates critical assets and makes sure that access is based on roles, auditors refer to IEC 62443. We should treat IEC 62443 as the NIST SP 800-53 equivalent for industrial systems. This will help us with threat modelling and selecting controls that are right for safety-critical operations.

MISP

Malware Information Sharing Platform

MISP lets us share and use Indicators of Compromise, adversary profiles and threat-actor campaigns when we're part of threat-intelligence communities. We create events in MISP containing IOCs, like malicious IP addresses or file hashes, and tag them with TLP classifications to control distribution. All that data gets sent to the SIEM and endpoint platforms, which help to improve the detection rules in real time. For example, think of MISP as the local community watch scheme. Its members share information about anything unusual they spot, and the rest of the community can then use this to protect their own organisations.

IOC

Indicator of Compromise

The IOCs we hunt for include artefacts, malicious file hashes, suspicious registry keys and known command-and-control domains, which signal a breach. So, the endpoint detection system scans file systems for these hashes, and network sensors match DNS requests against IOC lists. When there's an incident, the responders collect information from threat intelligence feeds and forensic images, and then they look at how the attackers moved. If you think about it, IOCs are like digital fingerprints left at a crime scene: if we can find a match, we can identify the perpetrator and see how bad the damage is.

TIP

Threat Intelligence Platform

When we take all these threat feeds from different places, like commercial providers, open-source projects and our own internal reports, and combine them, a threat intelligence platform makes things much easier. Then we configure TIP to deduplicate indicators, score feed reliability and map data to standardised schemas like STIX2. The alerts are based on context, location, industry and so on, and they help the team to decide what to investigate first. When you integrate it with ticketing systems, it automatically adds IOC details and threat actor profiles to the alerts.

YARA

Yet Another Ridiculous Acronym

One of the things we do is to design custom malware-detection rules, and YARA patterns let us match on binary strings, file metadata and logical expressions. We use YARA rules to spot specific families, like banking trojans or cryptominers, in endpoint scans. It's like, security researchers come up with these YARA rule sets when they're analysing malware, and they spot unique byte sequences or PE header anomalies. These rules are then sent to the EDR and sandbox environments by automated pipelines, which flag new samples for more detailed checking.

CTI

Cyber Threat Intelligence

We can get more strategic by looking at attacker motivations and infrastructure, and that's where cyber threat intelligence comes in. We're also into CTI feeds that profile threat actors, TTPs, targeted industries and observed campaigns, and map them to frameworks like MITRE ATT&CK. The tools help us to link indicators with the IDs of the groups we're up against, so we can work out what the attackers will do next. It also informs phishing simulations, red-team exercises and control validations, so that the defences match up with the actual threat landscapes. It's like the daily briefing that the team uses to stay one step ahead of the bad guys, setting rules for what to look out for now and planning for security in the long term.

NACRM

Network Access Control and Risk Management

When we check device posture before allowing network access, NACRM frameworks integrate NAC systems with risk-management workflows. The NAC solution checks endpoint health, patch levels, AV status and configuration compliance, and gives risk scores that determine VLAN placement or quarantine policies. The risk managers check the overall posture data to spot trends, like which OS versions are at risk across the network, and then set off automated patch deployment campaigns.

ODR

On-Demand Remediation

Whenever continuous monitoring flags a problem, on-demand remediation tools let us apply fixes straight away, like disabling a risky service or updating a firewall rule, without waiting for the next maintenance window. What we do is integrate ODR scripts with the orchestration platform, so you can deploy patches or configuration changes across multiple servers with just one click. There are real-time dashboards that show you the remediation status and compliance gains. To put it simply, ODR is like a fire suppression system that automatically releases water when it detects flames, stopping small fires before they turn into big ones.

SOAR

Security Orchestration, Automation and Response

The SOAR platform is great because it can automate repetitive tasks, add IOC data to alerts, block malicious IPs on firewalls and open incident-response tickets. Their playbooks are like workflows that outline how to handle specific situations, getting all the relevant tools and teams on the same page. We measure how well our playbooks are working by looking at how much the mean time to respond (MTTR) goes down and how much analyst capacity goes up. And if you're thinking about SOAR integration, you'll be glad to hear that it helps the organisation react faster than its rivals can adapt.

STIX2

Structured Threat Information eXpression (Version 2)

If we share threat intelligence within the organisation or with trusted partners, STIX2 provides a standardised JSON schema for expressing indicators, attack patterns, threat actors and relationships. Then we package enriched CTI, IOCs, malware signatures and campaign timelines into STIX2 bundles, making sure they're all parsed consistently across TIPs, SIEMs and SOAR platforms. The system automatically updates the detection rules and playbooks in real time. If you think about STIX2 as the go-to file format for threat data, you'll see that it makes sure everyone's on the same page, no matter what system or team they're working with.

Knowledge Check

1. When we see an identifier like "CVE-2025-0478" in a scanner report, what does it represent?
   - A. A severity score from 0.0 to 10.0
   - B. A rule for automated patch deployment
   - C. A standardized vulnerability description in the public catalog
   - D. A weakness classification for coding errors

2. A CVSS base score of 9.8 indicates what about a vulnerability?
   - A. It only affects legacy industrial control systems under IEC 62443
   - B. It is a common weakness that developers should avoid
   - C. It can be safely deferred because it is low risk
   - D. It requires immediate attention due to high exploitability and impact

3. Mapping CVEs to CWE entries helps you:
   - A. Automate ticket creation in the orchestration tool
   - B. Share indicators with partner organizations
   - C. Identify the underlying flaw patterns for secure-coding training
   - D. Quantify financial impact via ALE

4. Which database enriches CVE entries with detailed metadata and JSON feeds?
   - A. TIP
   - B. OVAL
   - C. NVD
   - D. MISP

5. When automating configuration checks across Windows and Linux, which language format do we use?
   - A. YARA rules
   - B. OVAL definitions
   - C. SOAR playbooks
   - D. STIX2 bundles

6. An industrial plant follows IEC 62443 guidelines primarily to secure:
   - A. Cloud-native microservices
   - B. Operational technology and control-system networks
   - C. Public-facing web applications

D. Enterprise social-networking platforms

7. We receive a feed of IP addresses and file hashes labeled as malicious. Which acronym describes these data points?
A. NACRM
B. CVSS
C. ODR
D. IOC

8. A threat-intelligence platform (TIP) helps us to:
A. Execute on-demand remediation scripts across servers
B. Rate vulnerability severity on a 0–10 scale
C. Aggregate and score multiple intelligence feeds for relevance
D. Define cross-site request-forgery tokens in web forms

9. When we write patterns to detect specific malware families in files, we use:
A. STIX2 schemas
B. YARA rules
C. SOAR playbooks
D. CVE IDs

10. Automating the incident-response runbooks and integrating detection tools is the role of:
A. CWE
B. SOAR
C. OVAL
D. ALE

Answer Key:

1. C

2. D

3. C

4. C

5. B

6. B

7. D

8. C

9. B

10. B

Reconnaissance & Social Engineering

The smartest opponents start by getting information and messing with people instead of machines. In this section, we'll look at how attackers check if people are real with CAPTCHA challenges, steal sensitive data like health information and personal details, and use instant messaging platforms for SPIM. There are a few things to bear in mind when it comes to email protocols. SMTP and its secure variant SMTPS are used for both legitimate communications and phishing campaigns. So, if you do a WHOIS lookup, you can find out all sorts of stuff about a domain, and sometimes that can be used in social engineering scams. And we'll see how all these elements fit into threat modelling, phishing simulations, compliance assessments and early-warning systems. This helps us strengthen our technical and human defences before attacker's strike.

CAPTCHA

Completely Automated Public Turing Test to Tell Computers and Humans Apart

A CAPTCHA challenge is a way of stopping bots from abusing online forms and account creation workflows. When we add CAPTCHA to the login or comment pages, users must either recognise distorted text or select images that match a prompt, proving they're human. Their security teams find the right balance between accessibility and bot mitigation by setting audio challenges for visually impaired users. But attackers are getting wise to this, using machine-learning solvers to beat the system. So we're keeping an eye on failure rates and changing CAPTCHA styles on the regular.

PHI

Protected Health Information

According to healthcare regulations, any data element that identifies a patient or relates to their health status counts as PHI. The way we audit electronic medical-record systems is to make sure they have encryption at rest and in transit, strict access controls and comprehensive audit logging. When we design intake forms, we make sure we only collect the data we need for treatment, so we minimise PHI exposure. The plans say that we need to tell the regulators and affected patients straight away if there's a breach, as the law says we must. We need to treat PHI as the crown jewels of healthcare data. If it's compromised, both patient privacy and institutional trust suffer, so we must act quickly to contain and remediate any disclosure.

PII

Personally Identifiable Information

Information that can identify someone in a unique way, like their name, address, email or social security number, is PII. We do these data-flow mapping exercises to find PII across databases, logs and backups. It's all about privacy by design, with developers getting to grips with pseudonymisation and redaction of PII before analytics processes. These security teams make sure that only the right people can see sensitive records by having different levels of access and automatically closing sessions after a certain time. When a breach occurs, the laws about notifying people about their personal information can be different depending on where you are, so we've got an incident-response checklist that's based on the local rules.

SPIM

Spam over Instant Messaging

There are a lot of people on chat platforms who receive unsolicited messages from attackers with phishing links or malicious files. We set up the enterprise IM gateway to scan all attachments and URLs, and block those that match SPIM patterns. So, user education campaigns teach employees to be careful of any requests that seem a bit weird, even if they come from people they know and think are safe. This feature uses real-time analytics to spot identical messages across channels and automatically quarantine the sender. In the company chat app, SPIM is like junk mail: if you don't keep an eye on it, it'll distract your users and deliver malware, so we take it as seriously as email spam.

SMTP

Simple Mail Transfer Protocol

SMTP is what's used to route email between mail servers. When we set up outgoing mail for the domain, we enter the SMTP server addresses and authentication credentials so that only authorised systems can send on behalf of the organisation. But attackers are using open SMTP relays to send mass phishing or spam campaigns from addresses that look legitimate. So, we make sure the servers are secure by doing things like making SMTP authentication a must, turning down messages from unknown sources and keeping an eye on bounce rates.

SMTPS

SMTP over Secure Socket Layer

SMTPS encrypts the SMTP session using TLS so that login credentials and email content remain confidential during transmission. We can enable SMTPS on port 465 or upgrade SMTP connections with StartTLS commands. The mail clients and servers negotiate certificates before sending or receiving messages, so attackers can't eavesdrop on or alter the mail as it's going through. It's often the case that data privacy compliance standards require all email exchanges to use SMTPS.

WHOIS

Domain Registration Lookup

A WHOIS query gives you the lowdown on who owns a domain name, like the registrant's name, company, email address, and when it was registered. We might see that a suspicious domain was registered a few days ago with fake contact information, which is a classic sign of phishing or command-and-control infrastructure. The security teams automate WHOIS lookups as part of threat intelligence enrichment, feeding the results into TIPs and SOAR playbooks. We also keep an eye on WHOIS records to spot any unauthorised changes or expirations that could lead to domain hijacking. Just treat WHOIS as the public record for the domain. If you do that, you'll be helping us spot fraudulent domains and secure the brand reputation.

Knowledge Check

1. Which control helps us block automated scripts from submitting forms on the website?

A. PHI
B. CAPTCHA
C. WHOIS
D. SPIM

2. A HIPAA-regulated healthcare system stores patient diagnoses and treatment dates. Which acronym refers to that data?

A. PII
B. PHI
C. SMTP
D. OVAL

3. An employee's date of birth and email address stored in the CRM are examples of:

A. CAPTCHA
B. PII
C. RFI
D. DEP

4. The corporate chat platform begins receiving unsolicited messages with phishing links. This is known as:

A. SPIM
B. SQLi
C. DDoS
D. ROP

5. We configure the mail server on port 25 and require authentication for outbound mail.

Which protocol have we secured?

A. SMTPS
B. SMTP
C. CSRF
D. LFI

6. To ensure email credentials and contents remain confidential in transit, we enable:
   A. SMTP
   B. SPIM
   C. SMTPS
   D. WHOIS

7. Before sending a phishing simulation, we verify target domains' registration details using:
   A. ODR
   B. NVD
   C. WHOIS
   D. CTI

8. A marketing form includes a distorted-text challenge that users must solve before submission. This test is called:
   A. PHI
   B. PII
   C. CAPTCHA
   D. IEC 62443

9. Which data type requires us to follow both privacy-by-design and data-subject access request workflows?
   A. SPIM
   B. SMTP
   C. PHI and PII
   D. DEP

10. The mail-gateway filters enforce TLS encryption on port 465. Which secure protocol are we using?
    A. SMTP
    B. SMTPS
    C. CSRF
    D. BASH

Answer Key:

1. B

2. B
3. B
4. A
5. B
6. C
7. C
8. C
9. C
10. B

Detection & Mitigation Tools

A strong defence is all about blending human expertise with automated systems that work together. We usually rely on specialist teams, like the CERT and CIRT, to handle incidents. There's Data Loss Prevention (DLP) to stop sensitive information from getting out, and Endpoint Detection and Response (EDR) to spot any unusual activity on each device. Then, there are host- and network-based sensors (HIDS, HIPS, NIDS, NIPS) which catch anomalies at different points. And finally, there are Next-Generation Firewalls (NGFW) and Web Application Firewalls (WAF), which enforce policies at the perimeter and application layers. Also, there's a SIEM platform that brings together alerts from all these sources, and the XDR, which puts them all into one place so that we can spot and deal with threats faster and more accurately.

CERT

Computer Emergency Response Team

CERT is the organisation's central hub for vulnerability advisories and rapid coordination. The analysts at CERT collect threat intelligence feeds and check new vulnerability disclosures before issuing clear, actionable bulletins. We count on them to help us schedule patch deployments, update detection signatures and train stakeholders on emerging risks. There are regular drills run by the CERT to test the cross-team communication channels, making sure that sysadmins, developers and executives all receive the same instructions at the same time. To put it simply, the CERT is like the cybersecurity dispatch centre, directing every responder to the right resources and reference materials when the next zero-day emerges.

CIRT

Computer Incident Response Team

When there's a breach, the CIRT gets going on a plan for how to deal with it. So, the forensics experts and network engineers work together, and they do things like isolating the affected parts, collecting memory artefacts and replaying attack chains. The plan is to follow the CIRT's playbook, which involves containment, eradication and recovery, while legal and PR advisers prepare notifications. Once everything's back to normal, the CIRT leads a session where we talk about what we've learned, update the controls and polish the future runbooks.

DLP

Data Loss Prevention

We all know how important it is to keep critical data, customer records and financial reports safe, which is why you need a DLP solution that can inspect content at rest, in motion and in use. The DLP policies spot patterns like credit card numbers or proprietary formulas, and blocks or encrypts them when users try to email, upload or copy to USB drives. We set up exception rules for approved workflows, striking a balance between security and productivity. The DLP generates alerts which then flow into the SIEM, where we correlate them with user behaviour and detect insider threats.

EDR

Endpoint Detection and Response

On each workstation and server, the EDR agent records process creations, file modifications and network connections as they happen. We make detection rules to spot unusual activity, like PowerShell invoking remote downloads and unknown DLL injections, which traditional antivirus software might miss. When an alert fires, the EDR console lets us isolate the machine, terminate malicious processes and roll back changes. You can also use historical telemetry to do in-depth analysis, showing the exact order of events. You should treat EDR like a health-monitoring system for the endpoints. It catches infections in their earliest stages and gives us the tools to respond surgically.

HIDS

Host-Based Intrusion Detection System

A HIDS agent installed on each server keeps an eye on system logs, configuration files and registry settings. We've got rules in place to spot anything unusual, like changes, new accounts for admin users, or changes to firewall policies, as these could be a sign of a breach. It puts all the alerts together so we can spot patterns across hosts, like changes that happen at the same time, which could mean an organised attack. To put it simply, HIDS is like a personal guard for your machines. It'll let you know right away if someone tries to mess with your most important files.

HIPS

Host-Based Intrusion Prevention System

HIPS is based on HIDS, but it actively stops malicious actions in their tracks. These HIPS policies stop unapproved binaries being executed, block privilege-escalation exploits and intercept known exploit signatures in memory. It works with the patch system and EDR, so HIPS can adapt its rules as new vulnerabilities appear and close threat paths. HIPS acts like a host that can defend itself. It spots intruders, locks the doors to keep them out and even undoes their footprints.

NIDS

Network-Based Intrusion Detection System

The NIDS sensors are put in place at network chokepoints, and they check mirrored traffic for known attack patterns, SQL injection attempts or probes of the network. The NIDS appliances monitor both inbound and east-west flows, so you can be sure no data is being missed. Any anomalies that pop up trigger alerts that go into the SIEM's correlation engine, where we can trace multi-segment campaigns. The NIDS is like a ring of watchtowers around the network, with each one scanning its sector and letting the keepers at the central tower know what's going on.

NIPS

Network-Based Intrusion Prevention System

As for network traffic, NIPS doesn't just detect threats, it blocks them by dropping malicious packets or resetting connections. We come up with rules to stop port scans, exploit payloads and suspicious protocol deviations, and adjust thresholds to reduce false positives. It's all set up so that the threat intelligence feeds automatically update the signatures, meaning NIPS is always ready for new threats.

NGFW

Next-Generation Firewall

Essentially, the NGFW combines traditional packet filtering with application awareness, SSL/TLS inspection and deep-packet inspection. We write policies that allow for essential SaaS apps while blocking risky categories like peer-to-peer tools, based on user identity and time of day. The Sandbox integration analyses unknown files as they come in, and the IPS modules in the NGFW catch exploits at wire speed. You can think of NGFW as a smart security checkpoint: checking credentials, inspecting cargo and denying entry to unapproved applications.

WAF

Web Application Firewall

A WAF is a kind of security measure that sits in front of web servers. It checks HTTP requests for things like injection attacks, cross-site scripting and other application-layer exploits. We tweak the rules to keep out the most common OWASP Top10 threats, but we still want to make sure that normal users can still do their thing. So, behavioural learning modes adapt protections to traffic patterns, which means you don't have to spend as much time on manual rule maintenance. And the alerts from the WAF work together with the SIEM, so we can see any web attacks right away.

SIEM

Security Information and Event Management

The SIEM platform is smart. It takes logs and alerts from all the security tools it can get its hands on, and it normalises the data so it can apply correlation rules to spot complex attack patterns. So, for example, it can pick up on a phishing message followed by a suspicious login and lateral-movement event. Dashboards keep track of important metrics like mean time to detect and incident backlog. When you integrate it with the CIRT playbooks, it automatically creates and enriches tickets, so analysts can work from a single source of truth.

XDR

Extended Detection and Response

XDR is more than just endpoint visibility. It also collects telemetry from networks, cloud workloads, identity systems and applications, and puts it all into one analytics layer. And cross-vector correlation can show those subtle attack chains that might be missed by point solutions, like a compromised cloud credential followed by unusual data exfiltration through an endpoint. The automated playbooks kick off a coordinated response across tools, like revoking user sessions and isolating compromised assets. It's like an integrated defence orchestra, with every instrument, endpoint, network and cloud working together to detect and respond faster and more accurately.

Knowledge Check

1. Which team issues advisories for newly disclosed vulnerabilities and coordinates patch guidance across the organization?

A. CIRT
B. CERT
C. SIEM
D. DLP

2. A solution that inspects all outbound email, USB transfers and web uploads to block credit-card numbers from leaving the network is known as:
    A. EDR
    B. DLP
    C. NGFW
    D. WAF

3. When we need detailed, real-time telemetry on process launches and file changes at the endpoint, we deploy:
    A. HIDS
    B. NIDS
    C. EDR
    D. NIPS

4. Which technology not only detects unauthorized changes on a host but also prevents execution of unapproved binaries?
    A. HIDS
    B. HIPS
    C. IDS
    D. IPS

5. Inline devices that block malicious network traffic, dropping exploit packets before they reach the servers, are called:
    A. NIDS
    B. NIPS
    C. SIEM
    D. CERT

6. To enforce application-aware, user-based policies and inspect SSL/TLS traffic at the perimeter, we choose:
    A. NGFW
    B. WAF
    C. DLP
    D. XDR

7. A firewall specialized in detecting and blocking SQL injection or cross-site scripting against the web servers is the:
    A. NGFW
    B. WAF
    C. HIPS
    D. EDR

8. Centralizing logs and correlating events from firewalls, IDS/IPS and endpoints is the core function of a:
    A. SIEM
    B. CIRT
    C. DLP
    D. NSP

9. Which platform unifies alerts from endpoints, networks and cloud into a single analytics layer, enabling cross-vector detection?
    A. SIEM
    B. NGFW
    C. XDR
    D. HIDS

10. A rapid-response team that isolates infected segments, performs forensics and drives system recovery after a confirmed breach is the:
    A. CERT
    B. CIRT
    C. IDS
    D. SOAR

Answer Key:

1. B
2. B
3. C
4. B
5. B
6. A
7. B
8. A
9. C
10. B

PART III: SECURITY ARCHITECTURE

Network Segmentation & Isolation

A more precise enforcement of policies is achieved by dividing the network into smaller, more controlled zones. This prevents threats from freely roaming the network. We will gain an understanding of the ways in which bridges and tunnels, such as BPDU, GRE, and L2TP, maintain order and safety through traffic. While Network Address Translation (NAT) conceals internal topologies, segmentation tools such as Virtual Local Area Networks (VLAN) and Virtual Xenon (VXLAN) are responsible for the creation of logical domains within local area networks (LANs) and the extension of these domains across multiple data centers. Carrier-grade solutions, such as MPLS and SD-WAN, offer dependable and policy-driven pathways between locations across the network. Lastly, software-defined networking (SDN) provides us with centralized control over the dynamic segmentation of programs.

BPDU

Bridge Protocol Data Unit

When you've got a bunch of switches hooked up, you're basically avoiding single points of failure. The BPDUs flow between them all the time, carrying bridge IDs and path costs that help the Spanning Tree Protocol get rid of links that are no longer needed. Basically, we set up switch priorities so that the core switch becomes the "root," which makes sure that BPDUs send out and block any loop-making ports. When a link drops, BPDUs reconverge in milliseconds, reactivating a blocked path and restoring connectivity without causing broadcast storms.

GRE

Generic Routing Encapsulation

We use GRE tunnels to link two remote LAN segments over the Internet. These tunnels wrap the original IP packets inside new IP headers. We define tunnel endpoints on the edge routers, including the source and destination addresses, and set the MTU size to prevent fragmentation. The traffic between the sites uses this "virtual wire", which means it can handle multicasting and non-IP protocols that IPsec can't deal with. If we combine GRE with IPsec, we add encryption to the whole GRE payload. GRE is like a secure pipeline: it puts a protective jacket around the internal traffic, carrying it safely across untrusted networks.

L2TP

Layer 2 Tunneling Protocol

Have you ever thought about what it'd be like for remote workers to have full LAN access, as if they were sat in the office? The L2TP creates a Layer2 tunnel for PPP frames over IP, effectively extending the LAN boundaries to their devices. We usually use L2TP with IPsec, which is a good combination. The L2TP handles the tunnelling, while the IPsec encrypts the data. When you're configuring both the client and the concentrator, you need to use shared keys, authentication methods and matching MTU settings. This means that DHCP, NetBIOS and other LAN services can all work seamlessly at remote sites.

LAN

Local Area Network

The office has a LAN that connects computers, printers and servers over fast Ethernet or Wi-Fi. We divide this environment into VLANs, or logical broadcast domains, so that traffic from the finance department doesn't get mixed up with guest or IoT networks. You can boost throughput between critical switches using link aggregation, and Spanning Tree Protocol and BPDU messages help to prevent loops. The Quality-of-Service rules make sure VoIP calls are prioritised over bulk file transfers. The LAN is like the fast lane inside the building. By dividing it into clear sections, we make security rules clear, boost performance and make it easier to sort out any tech problems in each department's digital area.

MAN

Metropolitan Area Network

And if you've got a bunch of offices all over the city, you're probably going to need a MAN, which is usually set up with fibre rings or carrier-provided circuits. We make the MAN with redundancy, dual rings and separate POPs, to make sure it's always available. The MPLS services over the MAN provide traffic engineering and MPLS VPN segmentation, which separates different business units across sites. The MAN is great for real-time applications like video conferencing between branches because it has lower latency and predictable bandwidth.

MPLS

Multiprotocol Label Switching

The service provider's MPLS backbone offers fast, reliable connections for business traffic. So instead of sending each packet to every hop, MPLS gives it a short label that tells it where to send it next, which makes it easy to plan and predict how well things will work. We're asking for MPLS Layer 3 VPNs to split traffic into different virtual networks, using route-target tags to control which sites join each VPN. If something goes wrong with the link, automatic failover through RSVP-TE or LDP makes sure you're down for only a short time. The idea is that MPLS is like an express train network: once the packet gets its ticket (label), it follows a reserved track to its destination, away from all the other "passengers".

NAT

Network Address Translation

On the edge firewall, the NAT converts private IP addresses from the LAN into public addresses so you can access the internet. We set up SNAT so that employees' workstations share a pool of public IPs, saving on address space. For inbound services, like a web server, we set up DNAT (port forwarding) to map public endpoints to internal hosts. And with dynamic port assignments, a lot of our clients can use just one IP. NAT hides the internal layout from external scanners, reducing the visible attack surface.

VLAN

Virtual Local Area Network

What VLANs do is to let us divide the physical switch into separate logical networks by tagging traffic with 802.1Q identifiers. We assign switch ports to VLANs representing finance, HR or guest traffic, and we enforce access controls at the edge. The trunk links carry multiple VLANs between switches, with VLAN pruning to limit broadcast traffic. And with Inter-VLAN routing on a layer-3 device, you can control how your network is connected. This VLAN design enforces policy boundaries, meaning finance systems won't see HR's broadcast traffic. This reduces the impact of a compromised device and makes compliance easier by isolating regulated data flows.

VXLAN

Virtual Extensible LAN

If you're thinking of scaling VLANs beyond 4096 IDs or stretching them across data centres, then VXLAN is the way to go. Each VXLAN tunnel puts Ethernet frames in UDP, with a 24-bit VNID that supports millions of segments. We use VXLAN Tunnel Endpoints (VTEPs) on hypervisors or leaf switches, along with an EVPN control plane to share MAC-address info. And if you need to move your VM from one rack to another or between different clouds, it'll do that without any problems, and you don't even need to change your IP or VLAN.

SD-WAN

Software-Defined Wide Area Network

All the branches use various transport links, MPLS, broadband, LTE, to connect to data centres and cloud services. The SD-WAN uses a central controller to define business intents, like "prioritise VoIP over MPLS if jitter is less than 5 ms, else route via broadband." So, all the branch devices set up encrypted tunnels to the hubs, and then they route traffic dynamically based on how the links are performing in real-time. And we keep an eye on the links, tweak the policies as needed, and make sure guests are using different VPNs by directing their WiFi traffic through different ones.

SDN

Software-Defined Networking

Software-defined networking is a game-changer. In an SDN architecture, the control plane is in a central controller that uses APIs to programmatically configure forwarding devices. We're the ones who come up with the policies, define the segments, security groups and QoS, and push them to all switches, so you don't have to mess around with port-by-port configuration manually. Then there's automation, which handles VLAN and VXLAN deployments, while northbound integrations tie network changes to orchestrators and cloud platforms. And the controller gets real-time telemetry from the data plane, which means you can place workloads dynamically and micro-segment them.

Knowledge Check

1. Which protocol encapsulates the internal IP packets within new IP headers to form a virtual point-to-point link over the Internet?

A. L2TP
B. GRE
C. VXLAN
D. SDN

2. We need to extend a remote user's PC onto the office LAN so that DHCP and NetBIOS traffic work transparently. Which combination would we deploy?

A. GRE + MPLS
B. L2TP/IPsec
C. SD-WAN + NAT
D. VLAN + SDN

3. On the core switch, we observe Port-Fast ports blocking due to spanning-tree loops. Which frame type is responsible for preventing those loops?

A. BPDU
B. DHCP
C. ARP
D. STP

4. To segment guest Wi-Fi, finance and engineering traffic on the same physical switches, we implement:

A. NAT
B. VLAN
C. MPLS
D. MAN

5. After outgrowing VLAN limits, we need millions of isolated segments across the data center fabric. Which overlay technology solves this?
   A. VXLAN
   B. GRE
   C. SDN
   D. BPDU

6. The branch offices use broadband and LTE links in addition to MPLS. We want a centralized policy that steers application traffic dynamically across links. Which solution fits?
   A. SD-WAN
   B. NIPS
   C. HIPS
   D. MISP

7. A service provider offers us a carrier-grade backbone with traffic engineering and VPN segmentation. Which technology underpins that offering?
   A. MAN
   B. MPLS
   C. NAT
   D. OVAL

8. When hiding the internal IP addressing scheme from the Internet and conserving IPv4 space, we configure:
   A. GRE
   B. NAT
   C. VLAN
   D. SDN

9. Centralizing the network control plane and automating segment changes via an API describes:
   A. SDN
   B. SD-WAN
   C. L2TP
   D. NIDS

10. To create virtual LANs that span not just one building but multiple data centers over existing IP networks, we would choose:
    A. VXLAN
    B. BPDU
    C. GRE
    D. LAN

Answer Key:

1. B
2. B
3. A
4. B
5. A
6. A
7. B
8. B
9. A
10. A

Secure Infrastructure Models

These days, IT landscapes include on-premises data centres and lots of cloud services. We need to understand how each infrastructure model, from raw compute to fully managed platforms, shifts security responsibilities between us and the provider. The Infrastructure as a Service (IaaS) and the Metal as a Service (MaaS) supply the basic building blocks, while the Platform as a Service (PaaS) and the Software as a Service (SaaS) deliver higher-level abstractions. Infrastructure as Code (IaC) makes sure that everything is consistent and can be done again.

If you're looking to boost security for your users, Unified Threat Management (UTM) appliances and Virtual Desktop Infrastructure (VDI) could be the answer. The Virtual Private Clouds (VPC) are great at isolating network segments, and they use container-network interfaces (CNI), storage interfaces (CSI) and runtimes like CRI-O to power Kubernetes clusters. And of course, there's managed services, EKS, AKS and GKE, package orchestration, but we still make sure we follow pod-security policies, network policies and role-based access.

IaaS

Infrastructure as a Service

The idea behind IaaS is that you rent virtual machines, storage volumes and network components when you need them, but you keep full control over the operating systems and applications. We make sure IaaS is secure by hardening images, managing patch schedules and applying network security groups to limit inbound access. It's all about who's allowed to set up resources, and cloud-native monitoring keeps an eye out for problems like SSH ports being set up publicly. So, IaaS is basically like renting out raw computing and networking space. The provider provides the land and fences, but we're responsible for building and securing the buildings ourselves.

IaC

Infrastructure as Code

The cool thing about IaC is that the infrastructure definitions live in version-controlled code, using tools like Terraform or CloudFormation, which makes sure everything stays consistent across dev, test and prod. There are pull-request workflows, automated linting and plan reviews to stop drift before changes reach live systems. It's all about stopping insecure setups from happening, and we do that by putting security controls like default network ACLs, encryption flags and least-privilege IAM roles straight into the modules. You can treat IaC like a deployment blueprint. Instead of clicking through consoles, we apply and version the security-by-design patterns automatically, which means you'll be time-to-compliance in no time and any gaps left by manual processes will be closed.

MaaS

Metal as a Service

In situations where you need high performance or specialised hardware, MaaS uses an API to provision physical servers, just like IaaS does for VMs. We set up and cable the servers in advance, then use the MaaS portal to commission, deploy and disassemble nodes when we need to. There are security hardening templates and PXE boot images with preconfigured disk encryption and secure boot, which ensure that every server boots into a known good state. Just think of MaaS as automating data centre operations. It makes physical hardware as flexible and temporary as a virtual machine, but we still control firmware settings and hardware-rooted trust anchors.

PaaS

Platform as a Service

With PaaS, the cloud provider handles things like runtime environments, middleware and scaling, so we can focus on the application code. And we make sure PaaS is secure by configuring built-in authentication, enabling platform-managed TLS certificates and controlling environment variables that hold secrets. Things like network controls, service endpoints and private link connections limit your exposure to the public Internet. Application security testing is part of the deployment pipeline, so it can spot vulnerabilities before the code reaches the platform.

SaaS

Software as a Service

SaaS is when a software provider delivers end-user functionality, email, collaboration or CRM, while handling all infrastructure, updates and availability. The focus on security is moving towards identity management, enforcing SSO, multi-factor authentication and conditional access, and data protection via DLP policies integrated with the SaaS API. We audit third-party controls through SOC2 reports and configure session timeout and device-compliance checks.

UTM

Unified Threat Management

There are a lot of things to think about when it comes to network security, like firewalling, intrusion prevention, content filtering, VPN and antivirus. For all of that, we use UTM devices. We use UTMs at branch offices or cloud-adjacent networks to combine security functions, making management easier. So, policies are there to define what web categories are considered acceptable, block any malicious attachments that might come your way and enforce SSL/TLS inspection. All the logging is sent to the SIEM, which then puts everything together and looks at how it all relates. THe concept of UMT is like the security all-in-one toolbox, in which it puts a lot of controls into one easy-to-use interface, which is perfect for smaller sites or when you're first setting things up and don't want to get bogged down with lots of separate devices.

VDI

Virtual Desktop Infrastructure

In situations where there are regulatory or security concerns, VDI can provide guest OS instances hosted in the data centre or cloud. We use hardened group policies, antivirus and application whitelisting to lock down master images before spinning up pools of desktops. It's also worth mentioning that network-security policies and micro-segmentation help to isolate VDI traffic from other workloads. It also makes sure that the user experience remains snappy.

VPC

Virtual Private Cloud

When we set up a private network in a public cloud, a VPC gives us control over IP address ranges, subnets, route tables and security groups. We design public and private subnets, route tables for NAT gateways and interface endpoints for private service access. The flow logs capture traffic so it can be analysed forensically, and IAM policies restrict who can modify VPC settings. The VPC is the sandbox for all cloud workloads, and by drawing internal firebreaks, we make sure that only explicitly allowed traffic flows between tiers. This protects sensitive systems from lateral exploits.

CNI

Container Network Interface

In Kubernetes and similar platforms, the CNI plugin handles pod networking, allocating IP addresses, configuring routes and applying network-policy enforcement. We pick a CNI (Calico, Flannel or Weave) that supports the segmentation needs, setting policies to allow only the pod-to-pod and pod-to-service communication that's necessary. Plus, when you integrate it with service meshes, you get mTLS encryption and traffic shaping capabilities. Just treat CNI as the network fabric for the containers: it weaves every pod into the cluster network while making sure the segmentation rules we specify are followed.

CSI

Container Storage Interface

The CSI plugin provisions storage dynamically from cloud or on-premise arrays when stateful containers require persistent volumes, databases or file shares. We define storage classes with encryption, replication and IOPS parameters, making sure each volume meets security and performance SLAs. The access modes (ReadWriteOnce, ReadOnlyMany) make sure the attachment semantics are correct, so you don't end up with any data corruption. The CSI drivers work with secret management systems to securely provide credentials.

CRI-O

Container Runtime Interface for OCI

When we go for a lightweight container runtime in Kubernetes, CRI-O uses the Kubernetes CRI spec with the Open Container Initiative (OCI) image format. We set up CRI-O for read-only root filesystems, seccomp profiles and SELinux policies, making each container execution context more secure. We can integrate with CRI-tools to inspect images and enforce image-signature verification before deployment. For all you CRI-O fans out there, you'll be pleased to hear that it's just like the dedicated container engine. It'll run your pods safely and efficiently, sticking to both Kubernetes and OCI security standards, and it won't add any of the extra features you find in heavier runtimes.

EKS

Elastic Kubernetes Service

The EKS orchestrates control-plane availability across multiple availability zones when we manage Kubernetes in AWS, and we provision worker nodes or Fargate profiles. We make sure everything is accessible with IAM-based RBAC, VPC-native networking and AWS-managed encryption for etcd. The EKS-optimised AMIs come with hardened kernels and container runtimes. There are some AWS add-ons that make things easier, like the EKS-Distro of Kubernetes and managed

CNI plugins, which make patching and compliance a breeze.

AKS

Azure Kubernetes Service

One of the great things about using Azure is that AKS manages the Kubernetes control plane for you, so you can focus on other things, like node pools and pod security policies. You can also use it with Azure Active Directory for federated authentication, and with Azure Policy and Azure Defender to scan for compliance violations. The VM-based and virtual-node-based worker pools are great, and you can attach Azure Disk CSI volumes with encryption and snapshot capabilities. Plus, AKS's private clusters make sure that API-server traffic never goes through the public Internet.

GKE

Google Kubernetes Engine

Whenever we run Kubernetes on GCP, the GKE system automatically manages control-plane management, node auto-repair and cluster upgrades. So, we use GKE Sandbox (gVisor) to keep everything secure, with VPC-native clusters for private networking and Binary Authorization for image-signature enforcement. And with Stackdriver-integrated monitoring and Cloudflare WAF protecting ingress traffic, you can rest assured. GKE's autopilot mode makes managing nodes even easier by letting us define only pod-resource requests and let Google handle the rest. GKE is basically Google's version of managed Kubernetes, and it brings together deep integration with GCP security controls and innovative sandboxing to keep containerised applications agile and protected.

Knowledge Check

1. Which service model gives us raw virtual machines, storage volumes and network components to configure and secure yourself?

A. PaaS
B. IaaS
C. SaaS
D. MaaS

2. Storing the infrastructure definitions in Terraform or CloudFormation and treating them like application code refers to:

A. IaC
B. UTM
C. VPC
D. CNI

3. When we need bare-metal servers provisioned on demand via an API rather than VMs, we use:
   A. SaaS
   B. MaaS
   C. PaaS
   D. AKS

4. Offloading runtime, scaling and patching of application platforms to the provider describes:
   A. IaaS
   B. PaaS
   C. SaaS
   D. VDI

5. Delivering complete applications, such as email or CRM, fully managed by the vendor is the hallmark of:
   A. SaaS
   B. PaaS
   C. IaaS
   D. CSI

6. A secure appliance that combines firewall, IPS, VPN and antivirus in one box is known as:
   A. UTM
   B. VPC
   C. CRI-O
   D. GKE

7. Providing fully managed virtual desktops hosted in the data center or cloud refers to:
   A. VDI
   B. EKS
   C. CNI
   D. IaC

8. Isolating the cloud workloads within a private network, complete with subnets, route tables and security groups, occurs inside a:
   A. VPC
   B. UTM
   C. PaaS
   D. MaaS

9. In Kubernetes, the plugin responsible for assigning pod IP addresses and enforcing network policies is the:

A. CSI
B. CNI
C. CRI-O
D. SDN

10. When running a production-grade Kubernetes cluster on AWS with managed control planes, we choose:
    A. AKS
    B. GKE
    C. EKS
    D. CSI

Answer Key:

1. B
2. A
3. B
4. B
5. A
6. A
7. A
8. A
9. B
10. C

Resilience & Availability

Having services online means you need more than backups though. You also need to design systems that can recover themselves if there's a failure. We'll look at redundancy patterns like N+1, learn to measure component lifespans with MTBF and MTTF, practise fast repairs guided by MTTR, and define the business's tolerance for data and downtime using RPO and RTO. And if you protect the important boot sectors with MBR integrity checks, you can be sure that every server can restart reliably. All these concepts come together to create a resilience playbook that we can test with live drills, which confirms that when outages happen, the infrastructure bounces back without missing a beat.

HA

High Availability

One of the things we do when we're designing a high-availability architecture is to place extra nodes behind load balancers. What this means is that if a server fails, the service won't be interrupted. It's all about spotting unhealthy instances and automatically removing them from rotation. As we roll out software updates, we perform rolling upgrades, taking one node offline at a time, so no user ever sees downtime. If you unplug a live server and test it, you can see that traffic shifts to healthy peers without a hitch.

MBR

Master Boot Record

Just picture yourself turning on a server and then realising it can't boot because its Master Boot Record got corrupted. We can stop that from happening by automating MBR integrity checks, which compare the on-disk MBR to a trusted checksum each time the system is rebooted. If the script detects tampering or corruption, it restores the record from a secure backup. When you pair this with BIOS secure-boot, you can catch unauthorised changes before the operating system even loads. We treat the MBR as the keystone of the server's startup sequence, which gets rid of a critical single point of failure and guarantees that every machine can return to a trusted state after power loss or software updates.

MTBF & MTTF

Mean Time Between Failures and Mean Time To Failure

These are the mean time between failures and the mean time to failure. We use MTBF to predict how long repairable components like power supplies will last before they need replacing, and MTTF to plan decommissioning for non-repairable parts, like certain SSDs, before they fail. We can get a better idea of the replacement schedule by comparing the MTBF/MTTF figures published by the vendor with the actual failure logs. For example, if the disks have a 50,000-hour MTBF but start failing earlier, we adjust procurement to add spares sooner.

MTTR

Mean Time To Repair

There's no way to prevent every failure, but we can make sure they have a smaller impact by reducing the Mean Time To Repair. So, the first thing you need to do is to create detailed runbooks for each of the critical components, like network switches, storage arrays and application clusters. In the runbooks, make sure you include step-by-step instructions and staged spare parts. It'll automatically figure out what's wrong, right away, and let the on-call team know. We should also do regular fire drills to simulate hardware faults and measure how long it takes to detect and fix them. Viewing MTTR as the operational stopwatch drives continuous improvement, with each drill revealing process bottlenecks that we can then eliminate, making the repairs faster and the availability higher.

N+1

Redundancy Model

It's all about making sure we've got one extra of everything, like power supplies, fans, or database copies, so that if something fails, it won't bring the whole system down. We set up automated failover on these units, then check it by turning one off to see how the traffic gets spread out. The monitoring system will alert you if two failures happen at the same time, so you can respond more quickly. N+1 is like the infrastructure's spare tyre, just like keeping a spare tyre in the boot. This means that if something unexpected happens, we've got a ready-to-use "spare" component that'll keep things running smoothly without any interruption.

RPO

Recovery Point Objective

Defining the Recovery Point Objective means agreeing how much data loss the business can tolerate, measured in time. If we set an RPO of 15 minutes, the backup and replication systems must capture every change within that window. We use continuous data replication or frequent snapshots to meet this target, then test restores to confirm that we can recover to any point no older than the RPO.

RTO

Recovery Time Objective

The plan is to get you back on your feet as quickly as possible. The Recovery Time Objective is how quickly services must resume after an outage, for example, two hours. We design our failover architectures to cover all bases: we've got hot spare clusters for sub-hour recovery and pre-provisioned cloud replicas for multi-hour spin-ups. We can time the process precisely by conducting full-scale DR tests and failing over production traffic to secondary sites. We should treat RTO as the operational finish line: by practising and refining every recovery step until we consistently cross that line within the target time, we can guarantee that even major disruptions cause only brief service blips, keeping the SLAs and customer trust intact.

Knowledge Check

1. Designing the service so it continues operating when one node fails and automatically reroutes traffic to healthy nodes describes which concept?

A. MTTR
B. HA
C. RPO
D. MBR

2. We configure disk checksums and automated restoration of the boot sector on every reboot to guard against startup corruption. Which acronym applies?
   A. MBR
   B. MTBF
   C. RTO
   D. N+1

3. Planning to replace power supplies just before they fail uses manufacturer "hours-between-failures" data. Which metric are we relying on?
   A. MTTR
   B. MTTF
   C. MTBF
   D. RPO

4. A non-repairable SSD rated to last 1.5 million hours before failure references which statistic?
   A. MTTF
   B. MTTR
   C. HA
   D. RTO

5. Measuring how long it takes on average to restore a failed service from detection to full functionality refers to:
   A. MTTR
   B. MTBF
   C. RPO
   D. N+1

6. Ensuring we have one extra power supply for every rack of N supplies exemplifies which redundancy model?
   A. HA
   B. N+1
   C. RTO
   D. MBR

7. Defining that we can afford to lose at most 30 minutes of data in a disaster sets the:
   A. RPO

B. MTTR
C. MTTF
D. MTBF

8. Agreeing to restore services within two hours after an outage establishes the:
   A. RTO
   B. HA
   C. N+1
   D. RPO

9. Combining MTBF and MTTR calculations helps us predict overall system availability for SLA commitments. Which combination is correct?
   A. MTBF + RPO
   B. MTTR + MBR
   C. MTBF + MTTR
   D. MTTF + RTO

10. We simulate a data-center failure and measure whether backups and replica failovers complete within the defined time windows. Which two objectives are we validating?
    A. HA + N+1
    B. RPO + RTO
    C. MTBF + MTTF
    D. MTTR + MBR

Answer Key:

1. B
2. A
3. C
4. A
5. A
6. B
7. A
8. A
9. C
10. B

Data Protection & Privacy

Encryption modes, integrity checks and robust key management practices help us to keep your data safe. In this section, we're going to look at block cipher modes, CBC, CFB and XTS, which transform plaintext securely, as well as authenticated modes like GCM that verify integrity alongside confidentiality.

When it comes to wireless networks, CCMP makes sure your Wi-Fi connection is kept safe and secure. There are a few ways to protect data at rest, like Full-Disk Encryption (FDE), Self-Encrypting Drives (SED) and Windows' Encrypting File System (EFS). CRLs (Certificate Revocation Lists) are also important for keeping the PKI trustworthy. It's got Perfect Forward Secrecy (PFS) and cyclic redundancy checks (CRC) for extra safety. So, by mixing theory with hands-on demos, configuring LUKS with XTS, inspecting CRC checks and testing CRL updates, you'll build a privacy toolbox that protects both users and compliance requirements.

CBC

Cipher Block Chaining

Every plaintext block is linked to the previous ciphertext block using XOR before encryption, so if two plaintext blocks are the same, the ciphertext will be different. The whole thing starts with an initialization vector (IV) that makes sure you've got unique chaining, even for identical messages. CBC stops pattern analysis, but we're still on the lookout for padding-oracle attacks. We make sure we validate padding securely. For instance, encrypting user session tokens with CBC stops replay, but if the error messages are flawed, they can leak details about the decryption.

CFB

Cipher Feedback

As for the block cipher, we convert that into a self-synchronising stream cipher using CFB mode. Each ciphertext block gets fed back into the cipher's input, producing keystream bits that XOR with the plaintext. This design lets us encrypt data of any size, which is great for interactive applications like SSH. If a bit flip happens in transit, only a few bits will become corrupted before the feedback chain realigns. If you think about it, CFB is like mixing new paint with the previous stroke, where each stroke depends on the one before. So, if you change one stroke, it'll only affect a few that follow, and you'll find any errors in those.

XTS

XEX-based Tweaked CodeBook

In XTS mode, disk sectors are secured by applying a "tweak" derived from the sector number to each plaintext block before encryption, so identical data in different sectors doesn't produce the same ciphertext. We set up full-disk encryption tools like LUKS or BitLocker to use XTS-AES, making sure that disk cloning or snapshot attacks can't reveal repeated patterns. The XTS system has a dual-key structure that separates data encryption from tweak generation, which makes it more secure against targeted manipulations.

GCM

Galois/Counter Mode

GCM is a bit like a combination lock. It uses something called 'Galois field multiplication' to mix up data and make sure it's protected. To keep everything safe and secure, we use GCM in TLS 1.2+ setups and IPsec for both data and authenticity. The code handles nonces carefully, making sure it never reuses them, to stop forgery vulnerabilities from happening. The software automatically verifies tags and stops decryption if there's a mismatch.

CCMP

Counter Mode CBC-MAC Protocol

The CCMP protocol uses AES in counter mode for encryption and CBC-MAC for integrity, replacing the weaker TKIP. We set up the wireless controllers and access points to use CCMP exclusively, which forces clients to authenticate with strong encryption. The protocol's 128-bit key and 48-bit nonce fields make sure that everything is kept confidential and protected against replay attacks. But if you're keeping an eye on AP logs for CCMP negotiation failures, you'll spot legacy clients or rogue APs trying to downgrade. So, basically, think of CCMP as wrapping each wireless frame in its own secure envelope, signed and numbered to prevent both eavesdropping and frame replay.

CRC

Cyclic Redundancy Check

When we're getting ready to send a big file or packet, we work out a CRC value that the person receiving it can use to spot any accidental changes. The CRC is used in Ethernet frames and file transfer protocols, and it catches random bit errors, but not deliberate tampering. Basically, we use CRC along with cryptographic MACs, like HMAC or GCM tags, to make sure everything's legit. We can test the network with errors to see how well CRC catches noise, and fail-safe logic retransmits corrupted frames.

CRL

Certificate Revocation List

The PKI is kept secure by publishing CRLs that list serial numbers of revoked certificates, so clients can be sure to reject any expired or compromised certificates. The CA generates CRLs at set times and distributes them via LDAP or HTTP so that apps can get the latest updates. The system automatically checks the CRL during the TLS handshake, and if the CRL is out of date, it can block a legitimate connection. So, we balance how fresh the CRL is with how much we can scale it by adjusting the validity periods. You know how those "wanted poster" boards in schools? Well, CRL is like that, but for bad certificates. Clients glance at the board before accepting a certificate, and if their name is on the list, they'll politely decline.

EFS

Encrypting File System

On Windows systems, the EFS encrypts files and folders using per-file FEKs (File Encryption Keys) protected by user certificates. We back up EFS recovery keys to Active Directory to stop permanent data loss if users forget passwords. It's not a big change for the user, who can still unlock files at access time and unauthorised users can't read raw data on disk. If you test EFS by getting into encrypted files from an account without any special permissions, you can see that your data is still protected even if the disk is cloned.

FDE & SED

Full-Disk Encryption and Self-Encrypting Drive

There are two types of SEDs, software-based and hardware-supported. The software-based type encrypts every disk sector when you boot up, while the hardware-supported type handles encryption within the drive's controller. The software FDE offers flexible key management options and SEDs offload CPU work and provide instant crypto-erase by destroying the on-drive key. Both methods use something called pre-boot authentication, which uses a TPM or USB token. We've got drills that can recover encrypted laptops, so we can meet data-at-rest compliance.

PFS

Perfect Forward Secrecy

The PFS is used in TLS and VPN setups to make sure that if long-term private keys do leak, past session keys can't be recovered. Each time you do that, a one-time Diffie-Hellman exchange generates temporary keys that aren't stored long-term. The servers put ECDHE ciphersuites at the top of the list to make the most of elliptic-curve cryptography. We can see that clients support PFS by monitoring cipher negotiations and accepting connections. In simple terms, PFS works by shredding each session's key after use, so if the main vault of keys is compromised, it won't expose any of the one-time keys used for past conversations.

Knowledge Check

1. We want each encrypted disk sector to use a unique key tweak based on its location, preventing identical plaintext blocks from producing the same ciphertext. Which mode accomplishes this?

A. CBC
B. XTS
C. GCM
D. CCMP

2. To combine encryption and integrity in a single operation for TLS connections, we select:

A. CBC
B. CFB
C. GCM
D. CRC

3. On the enterprise Wi-Fi network, we enforce AES counter-mode encryption with CBC-MAC integrity checks. Which protocol is in use?

A. CCMP
B. CBC
C. CFB
D. XTS

4. When we need to detect accidental data corruption in network frames but not guard against tampering, we rely on:

A. CRC
B. CRL
C. PFS
D. EFS

5. Ensuring that revoked certificates never get accepted during TLS handshakes requires clients to download and check:

A. CRL
B. CBC
C. CCMP
D. SED

6. To protect file contents on Windows with per-file FEKs managed by certificates, we implement:

A. FDE
B. EFS
C. SED

D. PFS

7. When securing an entire drive at rest with hardware-based encryption and instant crypto-erase capabilities, we choose:

A. EFS
B. SED
C. GCM
D. CFB

8. Converting a block cipher into a self-synchronizing stream cipher for variable-length data uses which mode?

A. CBC
B. CFB
C. XTS
D. CCMP

9. Defining that each session uses an ephemeral key so that compromise of long-term keys cannot decrypt past traffic refers to:

A. CBC
B. PFS
C. GCM
D. CRC

10. To encrypt data-at-rest across every disk sector transparently via software at boot time, we deploy:

A. FDE
B. CRL
C. CFB
D. SED

Answer Key:

1. B

2. C

3. A

4. A

5. A

6. B

7. B

8. B
9. B
10. A

Service Mesh & Policy Engines

Microservices at scale is more than just basic networking though. What we really need is fine-grained control over traffic flows, security policies and observability. Services like Istio or Linkerd inject proxies alongside each pod, giving us visibility and control over east-west traffic without changing application code. So, policy engines like OPA separate the logic of decisions from the services, and enforce the rules centrally. And with vault, you can keep secrets and certificates under lock and key with dynamic generation and tight access controls. You can use Weave to network and monitor containerised environments. At the heart of it all, a Site Reliability Engineering (SRE) mindset ties reliability targets to operational practices, making sure that the mesh and policy layers meet the service-level objectives that have been defined. These will show us how all these components work together to secure, observe and govern the microservices landscape.

Istio

Service Mesh for Microservices

To get Istio up and running, we just deploy its control plane and sidecar proxies across the Kubernetes cluster, and it'll automatically intercept all service-to-service calls. Once we're set up, we'll define traffic management rules, like weighted routing for canary deployments, and set up mutual TLS encryption for every connection without messing with the application code. It's got telemetry features that record metrics, logs and traces, giving us a clear picture of dependencies and latency across thousands of calls per second. If a service starts to perform poorly, Istio's circuit-breaking policies kick in to stop things from going even further wrong. Put simply, Istio is like a transparent layer of traffic cops and watchdogs: it directs flows, enforces security and keeps an eye on health behind the scenes, so the microservices can focus on business logic.

Linkerd

Lightweight Service Mesh

Whenever performance and simplicity are the top priorities, we go with Linkerd. Its simple design is perfect for places where space is limited, and it adds just a tiny bit of delay to each hop. Once we've installed Linkerd's data and control planes, we'll enable automatic mTLS between pods, making sure that communication is kept confidential and authenticated by default. The built-in dashboard shows us request-level success rates and response-time histograms, so we can spot slow or failing services straight away. The service-profile feature on Linkerd lets us set custom retry and timeout behaviours for each endpoint. At the end of the day, Linkerd is a network guard that's as nimble as they come. It keeps traffic secure and supervised with minimal overhead, which is perfect for teams that are all about ease of use and speed.

OPA

Open Policy Agent

The Open Policy Agent is integrated as an admission controller or sidecar that evaluates policies written in Rego, its declarative language. Whether it's stopping unauthorised user actions, validating resource configurations or enforcing data access rules, OPA puts all the decision-making logic in one place. For example, we've written a policy that says you can't create a pod without putting in resource-limit annotations or specific labels. When requests reach the Kubernetes API server, OPA intercepts them, applies the policies and returns allow or deny decisions. Instead of putting rules into every service, we write them once in Rego and let OPA enforce them across the whole cluster. This makes sure everything is consistent and we can keep an eye on what's going on.

SRE

Site Reliability Engineering

The SRE approach is all about measuring reliability with SLOs and error budgets, and then matching operations to those targets. As an SRE practitioner, we make sure we don't overload the system by releasing new features at the right time. We do this by using things like blameless postmortems and capacity planning. When it comes to a service mesh and policy engine, we set SLOs for request-success rates and policy-evaluation latency, and we keep an eye on those metrics using the mesh's telemetry and OPA's policy-decision logs. When we run out of the error budget, we focus on reliability work, like expanding redundancy or refining policies, instead of pushing new features.

Vault

Secrets Management Platform

Vault is used to store and generate secrets like database credentials and TLS certificates, which reduces the risk of leaked keys. The apps authenticate to Vault via Kubernetes service accounts or AppRole, requesting short-lived tokens or credentials that expire automatically. The Vault policies restrict which services can access which secrets, and audit logs capture every access attempt for compliance reporting. When a lease comes to an end or a secret rotates, Vault will automatically update the applications without any downtime. It issues time-bound keys on demand and locks them away securely, so you don't need to worry about long-lived credentials scattered across environments.

Weave

Container Networking and Observability

And installing Weave's Net and Scope components gives us both a virtual network and real-time visualisations of container topology. What we do is use Weave Network Policies to control traffic at the pod level, which helps us to segment things without having to mess around with iptables directly. It'll show you live maps of the deployments, and highlight which containers are communicating and which ones aren't. When we're trying to figure out what's going wrong, we look at the live graph to see where things are getting stuck or where services are struggling.

Knowledge Check

1. Which service mesh automatically injects sidecar proxies and provides mTLS, traffic routing, and telemetry without changing application code?

   A. Linkerd
   B. Istio
   C. Vault
   D. Weave

2. We need a lightweight mesh that adds minimal latency and includes a built-in dashboard for success-rate and latency metrics. Which tool fits this requirement?

   A. Istio
   B. Linkerd
   C. OPA
   D. SRE

3. Enforcing Kubernetes admission policies written in Rego and centrally evaluating them at the API server describes the function of:

   A. Vault
   B. OPA
   C. Weave
   D. SRE

4. When we rotate database credentials dynamically and audit every secret access, we are using:

   A. Istio
   B. Vault
   C. Linkerd
   D. OPA

5. Defining service-level objectives, error budgets and practicing blameless postmortems are core activities in:

A. SRE
B. Weave
C. Istio
D. Vault

6. Which tool provides both container networking policies and a live topology map of the microservices?
    A. OPA
    B. Weave
    C. Linkerd
    D. SRE

7. We want to implement canary deployments and circuit-breaking policies across the microservices without modifying code. Which acronym should we choose?
    A. Linkerd
    B. Istio
    C. Vault
    D. OPA

8. A developer writes a policy to deny any pod creation lacking specific labels. That policy is enforced by:
    A. SRE
    B. Istio
    C. OPA
    D. Weave

9. Which combination describes a service mesh paired with a secrets-management platform for securing both traffic and credentials?
    A. Istio + Vault
    B. Linkerd + SRE
    C. OPA + Weave
    D. Spartacus + Galen

10. For visualizing real-time interservice communications and troubleshooting unexpected connections, we would use:
    A. Vault
    B. Weave
    C. OPA
    D. SRE

Answer Key:

1. B

2. B

3. B

4. B

5. A

6. B

7. B

8. C

9. A

10. B

PART IV: SECURITY OPERATIONS

In security operations, there's always something going on. This is the nerve centre, the part of the organisation that sees everything – monitoring, alerting, responding, and adapting as the world changes. It's like a 24/7 control room, with dashboards lit up and alerts flashing, and analysts working hard to make sense of every signal. It's not just about collecting logs for compliance, though. It's about turning millions of tiny data points into early warnings and acting fast to stop threats before they turn into headlines.

This section is all about the living system that protects the organisation minute by minute. Our "**Monitoring, Logging & Alerting**" service keeps an eye on things, pulling together telemetry from all devices, apps and clouds into one place, so you don't miss anything. "**Incident Response & Forensics**" is where things change from prevention to action—we chase down intruders, gather digital evidence, and learn hard lessons so we come back stronger next time. When it comes to "**Automation & Orchestration**", the hard work happens behind the scenes. Playbooks, scripts and smart triggers kick in, turning routine tasks and even emergency actions into fast, repeatable moves that save time when it matters most. The "**Identity & Access Management Operations**" team make sure everything is secure by managing every account, permission, and credential in the business. This means that the right people can get in, and the wrong ones can't. We use "**Service-Level Metrics & Reporting**" to keep ourselves on track. This means tracking things like uptime, response times, and incident counts. It's all about showing the business what's working and where we can make improvements.

Being on the security team isn't just about reacting when something goes wrong. It's about staying ready, learning from every close call and working as a team to make sure the organisation runs safe and strong no matter what's thrown at you. Each section is full of practical tips and advice, and all the acronyms you'll come across in the exam and at work. Immerse yourself and get ready for the real work.

Monitoring, Logging & Alerting

We can't defend what we don't see. This topic shows us how to collect telemetry, centralise logs and configure alerts so that every anomaly and every success is visible. We'll use APIs to collect metrics, put CWPP agents on the workloads and send data to an ELK stack for searching and visualisation. Plus, things like geofencing with GPS coordinates, time synchronisation via NTP and polling device status with SNMP all add to the data. We make sure we capture every event by standardising on Syslog and securing boot integrity through UEFI, while AIOps tools learn from patterns and an external CDN's logs reveal traffic anomalies. We'll work on defining KPIs and KRIs to turn raw data into useful business indicators and setting up alerts that let us know when something needs our attention.

API (telemetry)

Our system pulls application and infrastructure metrics through telemetry APIs exposed by systems like Kubernetes, databases or custom services. Once we've written scripts or used built-in collectors, we can then push these metrics into the monitoring platform. If you want to keep an eye on how healthy your system is, you can use an API to check the CPU usage, request rates or error counts every 30 seconds. When we're checking live dashboards, we can go from high-level throughput graphs to individual request latencies. It's like having faucets for telemetry APIs. We just turn them on to stream the right data into the observability pipeline, then keep an eye on the flow for anything unusual.

CWPP

Cloud Workload Protection Platform

We install CWPP agents directly on the virtual machines or containers, giving us process-level visibility and enforcing runtime policies in the cloud. These agents monitor file integrity, detect suspicious child processes and block privilege-escalation attempts. The CWPP integrates with the central logging system so alerts, like unauthorized binaries launching, become searchable alongside application logs. When we see a CWPP alert for a rootkit installation attempt, we cross-reference it against telemetry-API metrics to confirm whether that host's network traffic and CPU usage also spiked. The CWPP serves as the workload's security sentinel, reporting every critical event back to the operations team.

ELK

Elasticsearch, Logstash, Kibana

We centralize the logs by funneling them through Logstash or Beats into Elasticsearch, where they become instantly searchable. In Kibana, we create dashboards that correlate application logs, CWPP alerts and NTP-sync failures across thousands of hosts. When we investigate a slow-response incident, we filter logs by timestamp, host and error code within seconds. ELK's visualizations let us pivot from a heatmap of error rates to the exact log entry that caused it. The entire ELK stack is the log-analysis workstation, which can transform a sea of text into interactive charts and filters, and thereby empowers us to diagnose issues without hopping between servers.

GPS (geo-fencing)

We leverage GPS coordinates from mobile or edge devices to enforce geo-fencing policies that restrict access to sensitive data outside approved locations. By integrating GPS metadata into the telemetry stream, we configure alerts if a user's device logs in from an unexpected city or country. For example, simultaneous logins from New York and Tokyo within minutes trigger a high-priority alert. The geo-fencing protects against credential theft by making physical location part of the anomaly-detection rules.

KPI & KRI

Key Performance Indicator and Key Risk Indicator

We translate raw metrics into KPIs, like 99.9 % service uptime or sub-200 ms average response times, that align with business goals. Simultaneously, we define KRIs, such as five failed authentication attempts per user per hour or disk-fill rates over 80 %, that signal emerging risks. The dashboards highlight KPI health in green, while KRI thresholds turning orange or red prompt deeper investigation. When a KRI breach coincides with dropped KPIs, we know a risk event is impacting performance. It is the true business's speedometer and the KRIs are the warning lights, as both together guide the operational decisions and incident prioritization.

NTP

Network Time Protocol

NTP is used to sync our clocks across every server, switch and security appliance, so that log timestamps are in sync. If we point devices to redundant NTP servers, both internal and public, we can prevent single points of failure. We can get a full picture of what happened by putting together a timeline using time stamps. This means we can link CWPP alerts, API-reported metrics and Syslog events from different systems. We get alerts when a host gets too far out of sync by running regular NTP-offset checks.

SNMP

Simple Network Management Protocol

All the routers, switches and network hardware are polled every few minutes using SNMP to get interface statistics, CPU load and memory usage. The SNMP traps let us know straight away if something like an interface flap or a power supply failure happens. If you put these network metrics into the ELK stack, you can compare them with application-level telemetry, which helps you work out whether a service slowdown is due to server or network issues. And if you want to keep your network management data under wraps, you can set up community strings and SNMPv3 encryption. SNMP is the network's heartbeat, keeping us informed about any connectivity issues.

SYSLOG

System Logging Protocol

Our standard procedure for event reporting is to set up all servers and appliances to forward Syslog messages to a central collector. Whether it's a UEFI secure-boot violation, an SSH login or a Kubernetes audit log, Syslog's standard format makes it a no-brainer to ingest it into ELK or SIEM tools. We've got these parsing rules that we use to extract fields, timestamps, severity and facility. They also generate alerts on syslog fields that match 'ERROR' or 'CRITICAL'. When we get warnings about disk usage from the NAS via Syslog, we check them against CWPP and SNMP data to see if we need to expand storage or investigate runaway processes.

UEFI

Unified Extensible Firmware Interface

All new servers and workstations come with UEFI secure-boot enabled, so that only signed bootloaders and kernels run at startup. The UEFI logs any integrity-check failures in the system event log, which the CWPP agents and Syslog forwarder capture. When an unsigned module tries to load, UEFI records the violation before the OS loads, allowing us to detect boot-kit malware at its earliest stage. If you regularly audit UEFI event logs in Kibana, you'll always know about any tampering attempts.

AIOps

Artificial Intelligence for IT Operations

The monitoring stack is enhanced with AIOps platforms that use machine learning to spot anomalies, predict when capacity will be exhausted and even recommend steps to fix problems. If you feed telemetry-API metrics, CWPP alerts, Syslog and SNMP data into the AIOps engine, you'll get correlated incidents and less noise, so the team only sees actionable insights. When there's a sudden spike in errors reported by API and CPU saturation reported by SNMP, AIOps shows it as one incident with possible reasons for why it happened. To put it simply, AIOps is like an operations analyst with an AI twist. It sifts through loads of data to find the important bits and help us solve problems more quickly.

CDN

Content Delivery Network

Our ELK dashboards monitor global user performance by integrating CDN logs and metrics, cache-hit ratios, edge-server latencies and origin-fetch errors. If we're alerting on cache misses beyond a certain threshold, it helps us tune our caching rules and prevent origin overload. When telemetry-API reports traffic spikes, the CDN takes it in, but we keep an eye on the fallback rate to spot any origin issues. You can also use geofencing linked to CDN edge location logs to set access restrictions based on where the user is. The CDN is the first responder to user requests. Its health and logs are monitored to make sure static assets and API endpoints remain fast and reliable worldwide.

Knowledge Check

1. During a major holiday sale, the telemetry-API shows a sudden 5× spike in checkout errors exactly when global CDN edge-logs report increased origin-fetch failures. SNMP metrics on the origin servers show no CPU or interface issues. Which two areas should we investigate first to pinpoint the root cause?

A. CDN cache-miss and Syslog error patterns
B. NTP drift and UEFI secure-boot events
C. CWPP agent alerts and KPI thresholds
D. GPS geo-fencing and KRI spikes

2. An attacker attempts a brute-force SSH login from a country the policy prohibits. The GPS-based geo-fencing rule triggers an alert, but the CWPP agent also logs a new process spawn. To correlate these events, we forward logs via Syslog into ELK. Which query would best help us trace the chain of events?

A. Filter by source IP geolocation, then by CWPP process ID
B. Aggregate NTP offset anomalies by hostname
C. Plot CDN edge-cache ratios over time
D. Compare KPI vs. KRI trends for error rates

3. We notice that one of the database nodes is 10 seconds ahead of the rest, causing misordered log entries in ELK and corrupting audit timelines. Which combination of tools and protocols will we use to detect and correct this?

A. NTP for time sync and an AIOps alert for log-timestamp drift
B. CWPP for process alerts and GPS for location checks
C. Syslog forwarding and KPI recalculation
D. CDN performance metrics and SNMP polling

4. A rogue container begins exfiltrating data at low volume to evade detection. SNMP shows normal network throughput, and API telemetry for CPU and memory is within bounds. However, the AIOps platform flags a deviation in Syslog events that match a spoken CWE pattern. Which additional log source should we consult to confirm malicious activity?

A. CWPP runtime integrity logs
B. UEFI boot failures
C. NTP synchronization logs
D. CDN cache-hit ratios

5. The SRE team defines a KRI alert when the ratio of failed API requests to total requests exceeds 0.1 %. During a recent incident, ELK dashboards correctly highlighted the breach, but no alert was sent. Root cause: the telemetry-API tag changed from “status_code” to “http_status.” How would we prevent such blind spots going forward?

A. Implement schema-validation rules in the ELK ingest pipelines and enforce them via AIOps
B. Increase SNMP polling frequency and add NTP redundancy

C. Disable GPS geo-fencing and focus on CWPP alerts
D. Move to a different CDN provider

6. A zero-day vulnerability in the UEFI firmware is patched, but some hosts continue to fail secure-boot checks. CWPP alerts show those hosts running unsigned boot modules even after reboot. Which combined strategy will ensure comprehensive remediation?
   A. Use Syslog to aggregate UEFI secure-boot failures, then trigger an AIOps playbook to remount and reimage affected hosts
   B. Increase SNMP trap thresholds and reroute through the CDN
   C. Adjust KPI targets for boot success and ignore KRI anomalies
   D. Rely solely on NTP logs to validate firmware versions

7. You're troubleshooting intermittent log ingestion failures in the ELK pipeline. Beats agents report no issues, but NTP logs show large clock jumps, and Kibana displays gaps in timestamps. What sequence of actions resolves both timesync and logging consistency?
   A. Stabilize NTP across hosts, reprocess logs with correct timestamps via ELK's reindex API, then validate with a KPI dashboard
   B. Update CWPP signatures and restart the CDN edge caches
   C. Tighten GPS geo-fencing and revoke UEFI certificates
   D. Increase SNMP polling and disable Syslog

8. The CWPP platform detects unexplained file-integrity changes on several containers. Telemetry-API metrics show no CPU or memory spikes, but AIOps correlates those events with a surge in outbound CDN log exports. Which policy change will most effectively block this exfiltration vector?
   A. Enforce a CWPP runtime policy to restrict outbound SSL connections from containers, and add a KRI alert for large CDN-log-export volumes
   B. Disable NTP and rely on Syslog for timekeeping
   C. Enforce UEFI secure-boot on containers
   D. Raise the KPI threshold for cache-hit ratio

9. A compliance audit requires proof that all production servers synchronized their clocks to a trusted NTP source within one second of each other over the past quarter. Which combination of logs and tools will we present?
   A. SNMP interface counters, CDN latency logs and UEFI events
   B. ELK-stored NTP offset metrics, Syslog entries of NTP sync events and AIOps anomaly reports
   C. CWPP integrity checks and KPI dashboards
   D. GPS-geofencing breach logs and CRL fetch times

10. During peak traffic, the CDN edge-servers show increased cache misses, and API telemetry

indicates higher origin request rates. Simultaneously, ELK alerts on a KRI breach for error rate, and SNMP notes interface saturation on origin links. To automate the response, which AIOps-driven playbook makes the most sense?

A. Automatically scale origin servers via the IaaS API, prewarm CDN caches, adjust load-balancer weights and send a summary alert to the SRE team
B. Disable NTP to reduce overhead on origin links
C. Purge UEFI secure-boot policies to speed reboots
D. Turn off CWPP agents to lower network traffic

Answer Key:

1. A

2. A

3. A

4. A

5. A

6. A

7. A

8. A

9. B

10. A

Incident Response & Forensics

A good way to deal with an incident is to have a plan in place and do a lot of technical research. It'll be your job to follow the Incident Response Plan (IRP) to deal with any threats, collect evidence and get services back up and running again. Then, techniques from Digital Forensics and Incident Response (DFIR) analyse things like RAM snapshots and persistent logs from ERP and other systems. After Action Reviews (AAR) capture lessons learned, while special tools like EDR agents and AWS Systems Manager (SSM) help us gather artefacts remotely. All the little details, like CHAP authentication handshakes or the reconstruction of RAID arrays, are fed into the investigation. This makes sure that every step, from detection to remediation, is both rigorous and repeatable.

AAR

After Action Review

The idea is to get everyone together for an AAR once the systems are stable, so we can all reconstruct the incident timeline. Everyone chats about what worked well, like automated containment rules, and what hit a wall, maybe because the escalation paths in the IRP weren't clear enough. The facilitator identifies the root causes and improvement opportunities, and then turns these into a list of tasks to do. And if you write it all down, next time you do a breach drill it'll be a lot smoother and you won't miss anything out. It's like a debrief for incidents, where real-life experiences are turned into useful insights for making things better.

CHAP

Challenge-Handshake Authentication Protocol (Forensically)

The CHAP logs are checked during the analysis to spot replay attacks or attempts to access the system without permission. Each CHAP exchange produces a challenge-response record that we can match up with timestamped network captures. By recreating these handshakes, we can see if attackers are reusing old responses or messing around with challenge values. These tools look at the CHAP challenge and response pairs, which helps us to spot credential stuffing patterns and identify accounts that have been compromised. And remember, treat CHAP records as cryptographic breadcrumbs. They show how attackers tried, and sometimes failed, to impersonate legitimate users during the breach.

DFIR

Digital Forensics and Incident Response

Once you've got everything contained, the DFIR workflow gets going with disk imaging, RAM capture and collecting relevant logs from ERP, network devices and endpoints. We make sure the evidence chains are kept intact by hashing each artifact and storing them in a way that can't be changed. Then, forensic analysts use special software to recover deleted files, parse registry hives and reconstruct command histories. Meanwhile, IR responders use playbooks from the IRP to get rid of malware and restore trusted images. DFIR brings investigation and remediation together. It makes sure the team not only understands how the breach happened, but also prevents it happening again in future with decisions based on data.

EDR

Endpoint Detection and Response

In DFIR, the EDR platform is a key source for live alerts and historical telemetry. We use EDR logs to trace process trees, spot dodgy command-line arguments and get file-system snapshots. When responders isolate a compromised host, EDR's built-in forensics, such as registry-snapshot exports, provide a clear picture of attacker actions. And because we can automate these data pulls via EDR's API, we can get to the bottom of things super-fast.

IR

Incident Response

There's a clear lifecycle to IR activities that you've got to follow. So, you've got to be prepared, identify the problem, contain it, eradicate it, recover and then learn from what you've done. We get the IR team on the case, let the stakeholders know and put in place containment measures like network segmentation or account lockdowns, depending on how bad it is. When we're doing identification, we use CWPP alerts, EDR telemetry and ERP-system logs to scope the incident. The Eradication process involves fixing vulnerabilities and getting rid of any malicious files, while Recovery restores systems from backups that have been checked to make sure they're clean. IR is both a technical and organisational exercise: clear communication and decisive action are key to minimising impact and restoring trust.

IRP

Incident Response Plan

And the IRP documents the roles, responsibilities and escalation paths before any incident occurs. It sets out communication templates for legal, PR and executive updates, as well as technical playbooks for different attack scenarios. When there's a breach, we refer to the IRP to figure out which SSM-driven commands to run, which RAID arrays to image first and how to rotate CHAP secrets. When we do tabletop exercises on a regular basis, we can see that our responders understand the plan and can carry it out when they're under pressure. The IRP is like the incident roadmap, making sure that when things go wrong, everyone knows where to go and what to do.

RAID

Redundant Array of Independent Disks

Forensic imaging storage is all about considering RAID configurations, striping, mirroring and parity schemes, which spread data across multiple disks. We reconstruct the logical volume in the forensic workstation, putting each disk image back together based on stripe size and order. You can check the integrity of RAID with checksum comparisons, which stops misalignment that could corrupt critical evidence. RAID-aware imaging tools let us extract entire file systems or specific sectors for targeted analysis. To put it simply, RAID forensics is a jigsaw puzzle. Every disk image is a piece that needs to be placed in the right place to show the whole picture.

RAM

Random Access Memory

As the name suggests, volatile memory contains the live state of processes, network connections and loaded modules at the moment of capture. We use forensic tools to dump RAM from hacked hosts and analyse heap contents, memory maps and decryption keys stored in memory. This live-response data often reveals in-memory malware, rootkits or stolen credentials that leave no trace on disk. We look at RAM artefacts, EDR event timelines and Syslog entries to see exactly how the attack happened.

ERP

Enterprise Resource Planning Logs

The organisation's ERP system logs business-critical transactions, finance postings, inventory movements and user-access events, which can serve as forensic evidence when attackers manipulate or exfiltrate data. We can spot unauthorised changes to financial records or suspicious mass exports of customer data by exporting ERP audit trails. And cross-referencing ERP logs' timestamps with NTP-synchronized system logs validates the sequence of malicious actions. These dashboards help us spot unusual activity, like when someone has gained more access than they should have, or when a report is run that we didn't expect.

SSM

AWS Systems Manager

AWS SSM lets us run commands remotely and get forensic artefacts from EC2 instances without needing SSH access. We use SSM run-command to collect memory dumps, extract event logs and rotate credentials stored in AWS Secrets Manager. Plus, SSM's session manager lets us record interactive shell sessions for audit. If we define SSM-driven playbooks in the IRP, we make sure we collect the same artefacts across all the instances we manage, even in subnets that have been compromised.

Knowledge Check

1. During containment, we isolate a compromised VM and need to collect live memory for rootkit detection. Which tool and acronym combination do we use to acquire a RAM snapshot and then continue guided investigation?

A. EDR + AAR
B. IRP + RAID
C. ERP + CHAP
D. AWS Systems Manager (SSM) + DFIR

2. After eradicating malware, the team holds a structured debrief to capture successes and gaps. Which process does that describe?

A. IR
B. AAR

C. SSM
D. DFIR

3. We discover that an attacker used a replayed CHAP handshake to gain VPN access. Which forensic artifact helps us confirm the replay attack?
   A. CHAP logs + EDR timeline
   B. SSM run-command history
   C. ERP transaction records
   D. RAM dump + RAID reconstruction

4. The Incident Response Plan (IRP) instructs responders to image every disk in a degraded RAID 5 array. What must we do before creating a forensically sound image?
   A. Rotate CHAP secrets
   B. Dump RAM contents
   C. Reconstruct the array's stripe configuration
   D. Execute an After-Action Review

5. A high-value database shows unexpected record changes. To trace the culprit, we merge ERP audit trails with which endpoint data?
   A. EDR logs
   B. NTP offsets
   C. SSM patches
   D. AAR summaries

6. During remediation, we use AWS SSM to run scripts across hundreds of EC2 instances. Which IR activity are we performing?
   A. CHAP challenge verification
   B. KPI and KRI updates
   C. After Action Review
   D. Containment and artifact collection via DFIR

7. We notice an unusual spike in file writes just before the malware triggered. Which memory artifact should we capture first to correlate in-memory indicators with disk activity?
   A. AAR documentation
   B. RAM dump via EDR
   C. ERP export logs
   D. RAID rebuild logs

8. The DFIR team needs to preserve evidence of ephemeral authentication attempts. Which log source is critical for recording CHAP challenge-response exchanges?
   A. SNMP traps
   B. ERP transaction logs

C. VPN gateway CHAP logs
D. RAID parity logs

9. After recovery, we measure the Mean Time To Recover against the IRP targets. Which document helped we define those targets originally?
    A. Incident Response Plan (IRP)
    B. CHAP protocol spec
    C. EDR vendor datasheet
    D. AWS Systems Manager guide

10. In preparing for the next drill, we rebuild test environments using live-captured RAID disk images, reapply patches via SSM, and rerun the IR playbooks. Which combined practices does this represent?
    A. CHAP replay + SED testing
    B. DFIR + IRP validation
    C. ERP audit + RAM analysis
    D. AAR + KPI updates

Answer Key:

1. D
2. B
3. A
4. C
5. A
6. D
7. B
8. C
9. A
10. B

Automation & Orchestration

Sophisticated security operations are made more efficient by automated workflows and standardised configurations. In this part, we're going to look at how Infrastructure as Code, using tools like ARM templates, Terraform and Ansible, lets us define environments in JSON or YAML so that each deployment is repeatable and auditable. The idea behind Continuous Integration/Continuous Deployment pipelines (CI/CD) and RESTful APIs is to automate the whole build, test and release process. The SDKs and CLI tools connect these pipelines to the apps. There are a bunch of tools that can help with this, like Observability frameworks, Fluentd, Sysdig and Grafana, which can take in and show logs and metrics. Then you've got Kafka and RMM platforms, which handle event streams and remote management tasks.

ARM

Azure Resource Manager

It's a template-driven deployment model, so you can declare Azure resources, VMs, networks or storage in JSON files. We write parameterised templates that accept environment-specific values, then deploy them via the Azure CLI or portal. The resource groups make sure there are boundaries on the lifecycle, and ARM's idempotent operations make sure that if you deploy something more than once, it'll end up in the same infrastructure state every time. When we update a template to add security controls, like network-security groups or managed-identity assignments, ARM only applies the delta, so we can minimise risk. If we see ARM as the set of rules for Azure resources, we get consistency and we can stop things going wrong in development, staging and production environments.

CI/CD

Continuous Integration/Continuous Deployment

It's a set of tools that automates things like code integration, build validation, security scanning and deployment to production. The developers push changes to a shared repository, which triggers automated builds to run unit tests, static security checks and container image scans. Once you've passed all the gates, CD stages deploy artifacts to target environments, development, QA or production, using blue/green or canary strategies. If something goes wrong, rollback policies make sure that any failed release goes back to the last known good state.

JSON

JavaScript Object Notation

JSON is a lightweight, text-based data interchange format. It represents structured data as key-value pairs, arrays and nested objects. A lot of ARM templates, REST payloads and SDK calls can accept JSON documents, which makes it common in automation. We use JSON schema files to validate configuration templates, spotting missing fields before deployments run. When we're troubleshooting API failures, we look at the request and response bodies in JSON, and then tweak the parameters as needed. Basically, we see JSON as the glue that holds everything together, and we're pretty good at writing the right payloads and understanding responses in scripts. It all works together smoothly, with services and orchestration tools communicating seamlessly.

REST

Representational State Transfer

REST is an architectural style for web services that uses standard HTTP methods (GET, POST, PUT and DELETE) to manipulate resources identified by URIs. We use RESTful endpoints to interact with cloud-provider APIs and custom microservices, sending JSON or YAML payloads and receiving structured responses. The great thing about statelessness is that it makes sure each request carries all the necessary context, which makes scaling easier. When it comes to security operations, we might automate the steps involved in responding to incidents by calling REST APIs to quarantine hosts, revoke credentials or query telemetry endpoints.

SDK

Software Development Kit

The cloud or platform SDK provides language-specific libraries and tools that wrap complex REST calls into native methods. When we use the Azure or AWS SDK for Python, we can write code that provisions resource, manages identities and fetches metrics without having to hand-craft HTTP requests. The SDKs take care of authentication, retry logic and pagination, so we can focus on business logic. Then, we install SDK packages in the CI/CD agents and import them into deployment scripts or custom orchestration modules.

Terraform

Infrastructure-as-Code

It's an open-source IaC tool that uses declarative HCL or JSON to define infrastructure components across multiple providers, cloud, on-prem or SaaS. We write modules that bundle security controls, network ACLs, IAM roles and encryption settings, and share them across teams. With Terraform's plan-apply workflow, you can see the proposed changes before they're executed, which lets you review the differences and spot any policy violations. The state files record what's going on right now, so you can spot drift and make sure the team is working safely together.

YAML

YAML Ain't Markup Language

YAML is a human-friendly configuration language that uses indentation and simple syntax for readability. A lot of CI/CD systems, Ansible playbooks and Kubernetes manifests use YAML. We define multi-line strings, lists and nested structures without the extra quoting that JSON needs.

There are a couple of ways to catch format errors before execution: via JSON Schema or custom validators. When you're writing complex playbooks or pipeline definitions, YAML's clarity reduces mistakes and speeds up onboarding for new team members.

Ansible

Automation Engine

It's an agentless orchestration tool that uses YAML playbooks to invoke modules over SSH or WinRM. We're the ones who write the tasks that install packages, manage files and configure services, including security features like firewall rules or TLS certificates. They show common patterns, like hardening SSH or deploying monitoring agents, and include handlers that trigger on changes. And with Ansible Vault, you can encrypt sensitive variables within the playbooks to keep things under wraps.

Fluentd

Data Collector

It's a log-aggregator that's graduated from CNCF, and it uses plugins to collect logs and metrics from files, sockets or APIs and forward them to destinations like Elasticsearch, Kafka or S3. We put all the settings for the input, filter and output stages into one YAML file, and then we use grok or regex rules to turn the unstructured logs into something more structured. And even when the network's down, Fluentd's got you covered with its buffering and retry features. We add metadata, like host tags or Kubernetes labels, to events before we ship them, all for security reasons.

Grafana

Visualization Dashboard

It's a front-end for time-series databases (Prometheus, Elasticsearch), and Grafana lets us build interactive dashboards and alerts over the telemetry data. We define panels that query metrics, CPU, request latency or custom application counters, and configure threshold-based alerts that integrate with PagerDuty or Slack. And with variables and templating, you can use the same dashboards in different environments. To troubleshoot performance issues, we link Grafana panels to logs in ELK or traces in Jaeger to see what the root cause is.

Kafka

Distributed Event Streaming

Kafka is a high-throughput, fault-tolerant message broker that can handle a lot of data from telemetry APIs, CWPP agents or application logs. The producers publish JSON messages to topics, and then consumers like Fluentd or AIOps engines can read them in real time. It's got Kafka's partitioning and replication, which makes sure everything gets delivered in the right order and is durable, so you can replay it for reprocessing. We might use Kafka to buffer events during ELK back-pressure or to deliver security alerts to multiple subscribers at the same time.

RMM

Remote Monitoring and Management

All your endpoint agents for patching, configuration changes and script execution can be controlled from one place using an RMM platform. Basically, we define policies that automatically apply system updates, enforce security baselines and collect logs on schedule. When problems come up, RMM kicks in and starts fixing things using Ansible or SSM, rolling out fixes across the whole company. The dashboards update in real-time to show which patches are up to date and the health of devices, and alerts let us know about offline or non-compliant devices. It's like the operations remote control, extending the reach across every machine. It makes sure everything stays hygienic and responds quickly without the need for manual logins.

Sysdig

Container and Cloud Observability

A unified visibility platform, Sysdig captures system calls and container metrics to provide deep context for security and performance. We deploy the Sysdig agent on hosts or within Kubernetes DaemonSets, then define Falco rules that detect anomalous behavior, such as unexpected file writes or privilege escalations. Live troubleshooting uses Sysdig Inspect to drill into processes and network connections. Dashboards track SLO-related metrics and security events side by side. Envision Sysdig as a microscope for the cloud-native environment: it surfaces fine-grained details that complement the high-level dashboards, ensuring that we can both observe and secure every workload in real time.

Knowledge Check

1. The team needs to provision identical Azure environments for dev, test, and prod with built-in network-security groups and managed identities. We write a declarative JSON template and deploy it via CLI. Which technology did we use?

A. Terraform
B. ARM
C. Ansible
D. YAML

2. To automate container image builds, static security scans, and blue/green deployments whenever code is merged, we configure:

A. CI/CD
B. Kafka
C. RMM
D. Sysdig

3. We write an Ansible playbook in YAML that installs the Fluentd agent on all hosts, parses application logs, and forwards them to Kafka topics. Which two formats or tools are used in this workflow?
   A. JSON and ARM
   B. YAML and Fluentd
   C. SDK and Grafana
   D. RMM and REST

4. A microservice exposes a REST endpoint that returns telemetry data in JSON. The Python script uses the AWS SDK to fetch those metrics and push them into Grafana dashboards. Which three acronyms describe components of the solution?
   A. REST, JSON, SDK
   B. CI/CD, ARM, Kafka
   C. Terraform, Fluentd, YAML
   D. RMM, Sysdig, PaaS

5. We need to ensure infrastructure consistency across AWS, Azure, and on-premises. We choose a single, provider-agnostic tool that maintains state, shows diffs before apply, and uses HCL. Which tool fulfills these requirements?
   A. Terraform
   B. ARM
   C. Ansible
   D. CI/CD

6. To visualize CPU and memory usage over time, set threshold alerts, and drill into container metrics captured by Sysdig, we integrate:
   A. Grafana + Sysdig
   B. Fluentd + Kafka
   C. RMM + REST
   D. SDK + YAML

7. A developer writes a custom script to call an orchestration platform's API, waits for a response, then continues deployment. The script leverages the platform's:
   A. REST interface
   B. CI/CD pipeline
   C. RMM agent

D. Kafka topic

8. We want to stream real-time security events from Fluentd into multiple consumer apps, anomaly detector, data warehouse, alert service, while guaranteeing ordered delivery and replay. Which infrastructure component supports this?
   A. Kafka
   B. Grafana
   C. ARM
   D. Ansible

9. Automating routine patching, configuration baselining, and remote script execution on endpoints is handled by the:
   A. RMM
   B. Sysdig
   C. CI/CD
   D. SDK

10. In the CI pipeline, we lint both JSON templates and YAML Ansible playbooks, then deploy via the relevant SDK calls. This practice primarily enforces:
    A. Infrastructure as Code consistency
    B. Real-time monitoring accuracy
    C. RAID array reconstruction
    D. CHAP challenge logging

Answer Key:

1. B
2. A
3. B
4. A
5. A
6. A
7. A
8. A
9. A
10. A

Identity & Access Management Operations

Every secure environment depends on three things. First, we need to know who we're dealing with. Second, we need to know what they can do. And third, we need to know how to prove it. In this section, we handle core directory services, federation, certificates and advanced analytics that keep identities trustworthy and privileges tightly controlled.

We'll be looking at on-premises Active Directory (AD) and its certificate authority (ADCS), extending identity to external partners with ADFS and IdP platforms, and governing access through IAM frameworks that align with ISO/.../27 standards. And then there are the managed providers, MSPs and MSSPs, who support the operations. Plus, technologies like PAM, SAML, SSO and UBA make sure that privileged accounts stay locked down, logins stay seamless and unusual behaviours never go unnoticed.

AD

Active Directory

How would it be to walk into the office building and swipe your badge at the lobby? It's Active Directory's job to do that for the network. We manage users, groups and computers in a hierarchical structure, assigning permissions via group-policy objects that propagate settings across thousands of endpoints. When someone new joins the team, we add them to the HR group and give them instant access to shared drives and applications, while blocking everything else. The domain controllers automatically replicate changes, keeping everything in sync.

ADCS

Active Directory Certificate Services

When we install ADCS roles on Windows servers, we basically turn AD into a full-fledged public key infrastructure. We can issue certificates for TLS encryption, smart-card logon or email signing for users, computers and services. The templates define the enrolment rules, so only approved devices get certificates, and the auto-renewal workflows keep the certificates valid without you having to do anything. We can quickly invalidate compromised keys by configuring revocation via CRLs or OCSP responders. If we see ADCS as the internal certificate authority, we can automate secure communications, replace self-signed certificates and enforce mutual authentication across every domain-joined system.

ADFS

Active Directory Federation Services

We use ADFS as a federation gateway when we need partners or cloud apps to trust on-premises identities. We can map AD attributes (like email or department) to tokens that partners understand by configuring trust relationships and claims rules. All they must do is click a link, and they'll get a SAML or OAuth token from ADFS. That means they can access external applications without having to enter their credentials again. The ADFS farm uses SSL certificates from ADCS and syncs via load-balanced proxies for high availability. ADFS checks that users are who they say they are in AD and then gives them temporary credentials for outside systems.

IdP

Identity Provider

An IdP handles authentication for different apps, websites, mobiles and APIs, so we make sure everyone must follow the same login rules. We can set up SAML, OAuth or OpenID Connect endpoints in the IdP, and point applications to redirect users for single sign-on. Things like multi-factor challenges, session timeouts and conditional-access rules all run at the IdP layer, protecting every relying party equally. When you try to access an app, the IdP checks your credentials and MFA status, and then issues a signed assertion that the app trusts.

IAM

Identity and Access Management

What the IAM strategy does is define who can access what, under which conditions and for how long. We design role-based access control models, map business roles to privileges and implement approval workflows for access requests. There are regular campaigns to check that only active employees have access, and automated processes to fix permissions that are out of date. When it's integrated with HR systems, it makes sure that when new people join, move or leave, it automatically triggers the right grant or revoke actions. We see IAM as the organisational guardrail, balancing empowerment (getting on with your job) with protection (making sure access is always appropriate).

ISO SC 27

Information Security Management Standards

ISO publishes the ISO 27000 family, including ISO 27001 for ISMS requirements and ISO 27002 for security controls. We make sure that IAM processes, user provisioning, credential management and access reviews are all in line with these standards, and we document policies and map controls to Annex A. These audits check that we're following the Plan-Do-Check-Act cycle to make things better, bit by bit. And by following the ISO SC 27 guidance, we make sure we've got solid internal identity management in place. Plus, it shows our customers and regulators that our IAM operations are up to global standards.

MSP & MSSP

Managed Service Provider and Managed Security Service Provider

Once the team hits capacity, it's time to team up with an MSP to take over the day-to-day IAM tasks, user provisioning, password resets and patch management for both on-premises and cloud environments. Moving to an MSSP means getting access to some advanced services: We're on the case 24/7, keeping an eye on authentication logs, and if there's any unusual activity, we'll know about it straight away and be ready to respond to any credential compromise. The service level agreements define how long things should take and how often we should report, while making sure the team has enough independence means we can keep control of the strategy.

PAM

Privileged Access Management

For admin-level credentials, domain-admin, root or service accounts, we use a vault to store them and issue time-limited, recorded sessions. The PAM system automatically rotates passwords after each use, enforces multi-factor check-out and records keystrokes for auditing. These workflows give you access only when you need it and then take it away again automatically. It integrates with the IdP and SIEM, so you get alerts on any unusual activity by privileged accounts. When we see PAM as the superuser checkpoint, we make sure that the most powerful credentials never wander freely and that every privileged action leaves an indelible audit trail.

SAML & SSO

Security Assertion Markup Language and Single Sign-On

The SAML protocol defines XML-based assertions that the Identity Provider issues when users authenticate, telling service providers who they are and what groups they belong to. When SSO is enabled, we make things easier for users: with one login at the IdP, they can access loads of connected apps without having to enter any extra details. We can sort out SP-initiated and IdP-initiated flows, make sure session lifetimes are enforced and integrate MFA at the SAML layer. And SAML's signed tokens protect against tampering, while the SSO portal centralises user access discovery.

UBA

User Behavior Analytics

The UBA platforms take the authentication logs from AD, IdP and PAM systems, then use machine learning to work out what the usual user patterns are, how long it takes to log in, what order resources are accessed in and what device is being used. When something unusual happens, like multiple failed MFA attempts, sudden privilege escalation actions or logins from unfamiliar locations, UBA raises risk-level alerts. We use feedback loops to tune UBA engines, which helps to reduce false positives and highlight real threats. When we combine UBA with the SIEM and DFIR workflows, we can speed up investigations into potential insider threats or compromised credentials.

Knowledge Check

1. To centralize authentication across the organization and enforce MFA, we configure an IdP that issues signed tokens consumed by multiple service providers. Which two acronyms describe this setup?

A. ADCS + PAM
B. IdP + SAML (SSO)
C. UBA + REST
D. MSP + RMM

2. A new executive requires temporary domain-admin access that automatically expires after two hours, with all actions recorded. Which two technologies deliver this functionality?

A. PAM + AD
B. IAM + CSV
C. PAM + SSO
D. MSP + MFA

3. The organization must prove to auditors that user-access certifications occur quarterly in accordance with ISO SC 27. Which two acronyms are directly relevant?

A. IRP + DFIR
B. ISO SC 27 + IAM
C. ADFS + UBA
D. SSD + CDN

4. An external partner needs access to the CRM without copying user credentials. We configure a trust relationship using ADFS. Which IDM component does ADFS extend?

A. AD + IdP
B. PAM + SAML
C. MSP + MSSP
D. UBA + SDK

5. After noticing unusual login patterns on privileged accounts, we consult UBA analytics and find a spike in off-hours access. To contain immediately, which system do we trigger via the IRP?

A. SSM
B. PAM

C. CSV
D. Sysdig

6. The MSP handles routine password resets but must escalate any potential compromises to the MSSP for 24×7 monitoring. Which two roles do MSP and MSSP play in the IAM operations?
A. MSP: PAM rotations; MSSP: UBA analysis
B. MSP: UI development; MSSP: database backups
C. MSP: CDN management; MSSP: SAML assertions
D. MSP: IRP execution; MSSP: RAM dumps

7. A user logs in once but then accesses five different applications without additional prompts. Which IAM feature enabled this seamless experience?
A. PAM
B. SSO
C. CSV
D. RMM

8. We need to issue smart-card certificates to domain-joined workstations and automatically renew them. Which pair of acronyms applies?
A. ADCS + ADFS
B. SAML + SSO
C. ADCS + AD
D. IAM + UBA

9. A high-risk KRI breaches when more than ten failed authentications occur in an hour. To detect credential-stuffing, we integrate UBA with which system to collect raw authentication events?
A. REST API
B. AD + ADFS
C. CWPP
D. RMM

10. In a federated login flow, which component translates AD group memberships into claims for an external SaaS application?
A. MSSP
B. IdP (via ADFS)
C. UBA
D. JSON

Answer Key:

1. B
2. A
3. B
4. A
5. B
6. A
7. B
8. C
9. B
10. B

Service-Level Metrics & Reporting

We all want that the services must meet business expectations, and it requires more than raw uptime numbers. In this section, we will define, measure and report on metrics that align technical performance with organizational goals. We will explore the Key Performance Indicators and Key Risk Indicators that helps to translate system behaviors into clear signals for stakeholders. Then, there are Service-Level Agreements and Objectives that formalize commitments, while the Service-Level Expectations and Memoranda of Understanding can record the finer details. We will also explore the monitoring platforms, like Prometheus, and operational hubs like Network Operations Center that are able to capture real-time data. We wil also explore to calculate Return on Investment to justify reliability work and secure executive buy-in. All these elements form the reporting backbone, and helps to guide for continuous improvement and transparent communication.

KPI

Key Performance Indicator

Every team tracks a handful of metrics that directly reflect business value, those are the KPIs. We might monitor median API response time, page-load speed or transaction throughput. This thing begins by asking which performance aspect most impacts user satisfaction or revenue. Once in place, we build dashboards that display KPI trends, highlighting deviations from targets. During incident reviews, we refer back to KPIs to assess how quickly we returned service to acceptable levels.

KRI

Key Risk Indicator

Where KPIs show how well we are performing, KRIs warn of looming threats that could degrade performance or security. We identify metrics, like error-rate spikes, surge in authentication failures or low disk-space thresholds, that historically precede incidents. The implementation of KRIs involves setting alert thresholds slightly before KPIs breach, giving us time to act. During run-book drills, we can validate that KRI alerts fire early and trigger appropriate remediation playbooks. In addition, the visualization of KRIs alongside KPIs on a single dashboard provides a balanced view of health versus risk, and this gives us to be aware of not only how we are doing but what might go wrong next.

MOU

Memorandum of Understanding

This is quite simple. When two teams or organizations collaborate, there is an MOU that lays out responsibilities, communication channels and expected performance levels without the legal weight of a contract. Here, we draft MOUs before integrating third-party services, such as a shared CDN or joint-operated API, to clarify milestones, escalations and data-sharing agreements. In addition, the detailed review of MOUs gives uc confirmation that the evolving architectures or business goals remain aligned. In operational meetings, such MOU helps to resolve misunderstandings quickly, and thereby steering work back on course.

ROI

Return on Investment

Every reliability improvement carries a cost, new tools, infrastructure or engineering hours, and ROI quantifies whether the benefits outweigh these expenses. We calculate ROI by comparing cost savings, reduced downtime and increased customer retention against the investment. For example, automating a failover cluster might cost $50 k but prevent $200 k in annual outage losses. SO, if we present a clear ROI, it helps to secure budget for redundancy enhancements or monitoring platform upgrades.

SLA

Service-Level Agreement

An SLA formalizes the uptime, performance and support commitments we make to customers or internal teams. We define metrics, such as 99.95 % availability, and associated remedies, like credits or escalation procedures, if targets aren't met. The SLAs also specify maintenance windows, notification lead times and response-time guarantees. The monitoring of the SLA compliance requires automated reporting, for which, we configure Prometheus queries or log-analysis jobs that feed into weekly status emails. And after this, publishing the SLA metrics transparently helps us to build trust and set clear expectations for service reliability. The SLAs serve as both a promise and a contract, and thereby it aligns technical operations with customer needs.

SLE

Service-Level Expectation

While SLAs are formal, the SLEs capture more informal or developmental goals, such as reducing mean time to detect from one hour to thirty minutes. We document SLEs in internal playbooks or run-books to guide team priorities before SLAs are contractually binding. And, the monitoring of the SLEs often uses the same tooling as SLAs, but with different thresholds and reporting metrics. When engineers review their quarterly goals, they reference SLEs to focus on incremental improvements that pave the way for future SLA upgrades.

NOC

Network Operations Center

The NOC serves as the command hub where analysts watch dashboards, triage alerts and coordinate incident responses around the clock. Staffed with engineers who understand both KPIs and KRIs, the NOC follows run-books to escalate issues via pages or chat channels. During major incidents, the NOC lead maintains a live incident board, updating stakeholders on status, next steps and estimated resolution times. The NOC personnel can also be trained to read both high-level SLA compliance charts and low-level Prometheus metrics for rapid detection and consistent communication.

Prometheus

Metrics Monitoring System

The Prometheus collects time-series data through a pull model. It also scrapes the HTTP endpoints for metrics exposed. We add Prometheus client libraries to the code, export counters, gauges and histograms, and set up Alertmanager with KRI-based thresholds. When we use PromQL to query the data, we can build graphs to show trends in error rates, resource saturation and SLA compliance. When you combine Prometheus with Grafana, you get some cool dashboards for the NOC and engineering teams.

SOCKS

Secure Proxy Protocol

We use a SOCKS proxy to control access to the Internet when we need to, for example when getting dependencies during build pipelines. This means we can enforce authentication, logging and per-user rules. If you instrument the CI/CD agents or developer IDEs to route traffic through a SOCKS server, you can be sure that all outbound connections pass through the security controls. The logs from the proxy feed into the ELK stack or NOC dashboards show unexpected domains or volume anomalies. If we see SOCKS as the main point at which things get blocked for each app, we can see and control every connection, which makes the service better overall.

Knowledge Check

1. During a peak traffic event, the Prometheus dashboards show that the 99.95 % availability SLA target was missed for three hours, while the NOC logs indicate that no alerts fired. Which two areas should we investigate first?

   A. SOCKS proxy authentication rules and MOU clarifications
   B. KPI dashboards and SLE documentation
   C. Alertmanager threshold configurations and Prometheus scrape intervals
   D. ROI calculations and KRI definitions

2. The team invests $100 k in a new high-availability platform that reduces downtime from 10 hours/year to 2 hours/year. If the cost of unplanned downtime is $50 k/hour, what is the ROI of this investment?

   A. 400 %
   B. 300 %
   C. 600 %
   D. 500 %

3. We track API error rate as a KPI and set a KRI alert when errors exceed 0.5 % for five minutes. During testing, a surge of 0.6 % errors lasted three minutes without triggering an alert. Which misconfiguration caused this gap?

   A. Prometheus scrape interval set to ten minutes
   B. KPI threshold set at 0.7 % instead of 0.5 %
   C. SOCKS proxy logs not forwarded to ELK
   D. KRI alert duration set longer than five minutes

4. The formal SLA requires 99.9 % uptime, but the internal SLE for developing teams is 99.5 % to allow maintenance. A maintenance window extended service down to 99.7 %. Which statement is true?

   A. We met both SLA and SLE.
   B. We breached the SLA but met the SLE.
   C. We met the SLA but breached the SLE.
   D. We breached both SLA and SLE.

5. We and a partner company sign an MOU to share CDN capacity during traffic spikes. The MOU stipulates 24 × 7 support and monthly review meetings. Which two actions ensure compliance?
   A. Calculating ROI on CDN usage and updating KRI thresholds
   B. Configuring Prometheus to scrape CDN metrics and rotating SOCKS credentials
   C. Writing SLEs for CDN latency and building Grafana dashboards
   D. Documenting joint-support escalation paths and scheduling monthly performance reviews

6. In the NOC, analysts rely on a Grafana view of Prometheus metrics. When response-time KPIs degrade below 200 ms, the NOC lead escalates. Which practice ensures the NOC sees the degradation before SLA breaches occur?
   A. Updating SLA targets to match KRI thresholds
   B. Raising the ROI threshold for performance investments
   C. Defining a KRI alert at 180 ms in Alertmanager
   D. Adding MOU clauses for NOC staffing levels

7. Developers access external package repositories through a SOCKS proxy mandating MFA. Proxy logs show unauthorized egress attempts from build servers. Which two controls fix this?
   A. Expanding NOC shift coverage and lowering KRI thresholds
   B. Enforcing SOCKS authentication in CI/CD agents and updating Prometheus export rules
   C. Raising ROI on security tools and redefining SLEs
   D. Adjusting KPI dashboards and rotating MOU agreements

8. To monitor both performance and risk, the dashboard shows Prometheus-collected latency KPIs and error KRIs side by side. During an incident, KRIs tripped before KPIs degraded. Why is this ordering beneficial?
   A. KPI triggers always require remediation before KRIs
   B. KPI and KRI must both breach simultaneously
   C. KRI thresholds must be higher than KPI thresholds
   D. Early KRI alerts provide lead time to prevent KPI breaches

9. After a costly outage, we report to leadership that automating the NOC run-books reduced incident-response time by 50 %. Which metric best quantifies this improvement for the next ROI analysis?
   A. Number of KRI alerts per month
   B. Reduction in MTTR converted to dollars saved vs implementation cost
   C. Number of SOCKS proxy connections
   D. Increase in MOU review meetings

10. The development team sets an SLE to restore services within four hours for non-critical maintenance, and tracks this as an internal KPI. How does this practice support the external SLA of two-hour recovery for critical outages?
    A. Four-hour SLEs replace the external SLA once internal teams adopt them.
    B. Tracking SLEs and KPIs separately avoids any reference to the SLA.
    C. Meeting four-hour SLEs automatically extends SLAs to non-critical services.
    D. Training on four-hour SLEs builds processes that can be accelerated to meet two-hour SLA targets.

Answer Key:

1. C
2. B
3. D
4. B
5. D
6. C
7. B
8. D
9. B
10. D

PART V: SECURITY PROGRAM MANAGEMENT & OVERSIGHT

Managing a programme means bringing together all the strategy, planning and coordination. This is what you can see from the balcony. It shows you not just today's incidents, but the whole security journey: what's working, what's missing, and what's around the next corner. This is where policies become real, frameworks are mapped to how teams work, and every third-party handshake or contract is put under the security microscope.

In Governance & Policy Management, leadership sets the direction and makes sure everyone's on the same page. This is where standards, risk management and policy updates keep everything in line, whether it's a new regulation or a change in business priorities. Vendor & Third-Party Management is all about picking, vetting, and monitoring partners every day – because your security is only as strong as the weakest link in the supply chain. Every new vendor, cloud provider or service contract is checked for security. Audit, Assessment & Reporting makes sure everyone's on the same page. This is where we gather evidence, test controls, and turn findings into clear actions that keep the business honest and moving forward. So, whatever kind of audit it is – an external one, a compliance check or an internal review – the goal is always the same: make sure what's on paper matches what's happening on the ground. And Training, Awareness & Metrics reminds us that people are the heart of security. Metrics, dashboards and feedback loops help us turn lessons learned into steady improvement and real change.

This whole part isn't a one-and-done project. It's a living process, a feedback loop, and a team sport that brings together leadership, operations, partners, and frontline staff. This last part of the book is about keeping the ship on course, adapting as the world changes, and building a culture where security isn't just a box-ticking exercise, but an integral part of how the business thinks and works every day.

Governance & Policy Management

A mature security program rests on clear governance structures and enforceable policies that guide every decision. In Governance & Policy Management, we establish executive sponsors (CSO, CTO), define organizational standards (GPO, ISSO), and formalize relationships through contracts and agreements (MSA, SOW). Industry benchmarks, CSA STAR, FedRAMP, HITRUST, ensure we meet cloud, federal and healthcare regulations, while CSPs and ESG initiatives extend the program's scope to sustainability and vendor risk.

CSP

Cloud Service Provider

When we evaluate a CSP, we assess how its shared-responsibility model divides security tasks between us and the provider. We map the own controls, identity management, encryption, logging, onto the CSP's infrastructure offerings. Writing policy language that references specific CSP regions and services ensures that the GPOs apply correctly in multi-cloud environments. For example, we might require that the CSP encrypt all stored data and enable VPC flow logs by default.

CSO

Chief Security Officer

As a CSO, whether we wear the title or partner with one, we translate business strategy into a security roadmap. We lead the governance forum where program objectives, risk appetites and compliance requirements are debated and prioritized. When the board asks for updates, we present metric-driven progress against key initiatives. We empower the ISSOs and GPO writers to draft policies that reflect executive guidance, turning high-level mandates into actionable standards.

CTO

Chief Technology Officer

When the security program needs new tooling or architectural changes, we collaborate with the CTO to ensure alignment with the technology strategy. We co-sponsor sandbox projects, such as a FedRAMP-authorized cloud environment or a HITRUST-certified healthcare network, that require both security controls and platform evolution. By embedding policy requirements into the CTO's technology roadmaps, we guarantee that new platforms support policy enforcement from day one.

GPO

Group Policy Object

On the Windows domains, we use GPOs to enforce baseline security settings, password complexity, software restrictions, firewall rules, across every domain-joined machine. We test new GPOs in a pilot OU, refining them before wide deployment to avoid inadvertent lock-outs. When the ISSO updates password-rotation intervals, we revise the corresponding GPO and schedule an out-of-hours rollout. The GPOs act as the program's enforcement arm at the endpoint level, translating high-level policies into concrete configurations that keep every workstation and server compliant.

ISSO

Information System Security Officer

As an ISSO, or when we appoint one for each system, we own the day-to-day application of governance policies. We review proposed changes against the organization's SOWs and MSA terms, ensuring that every vendor deliverable meets security requirements. During compliance audits, FedRAMP or HITRUST, the ISSO gathers artifact evidence, GPO settings, risk assessments, encryption configurations, and presents them to assessors. You may assume the ISSO as the program's on-the-ground defender, translating abstract requirements into operational checklists, control implementations and audit packages.

Master Service Agreement & SOW

Statement of Work

When we engage third-party vendors, the MSA defines overarching legal terms, liability, confidentiality, breach notification, while the SOW spells out specific deliverables and timelines. We embed security clauses in both: requiring vendors to follow ISO SC 27 controls, permit penetration testing and adhere to the incident-response IRP. During contract negotiations, we push for rights to audit and continuous monitoring via CSP APIs or CWPP connectors.

CSA STAR

Security, Trust & Assurance Registry

When we adopt cloud services, we consult the CSA STAR registry to identify providers whose self-assessments or third-party audits demonstrate adherence to the CSA's Cloud Controls Matrix. We reference specific STAR levels, self-certification, third-party certification or continuous monitoring, in the procurement policies. By mandating CSA STAR-registered CSPs, we streamline the FedRAMP or ISO 27001 mapping efforts.

ESG

Environmental, Social & Governance

As ESG criteria gain boardroom prominence, we integrate governance controls, such as data-privacy safeguards and vendor-risk assessments, into the ESG reporting. We set targets for reducing data-center energy consumption, mandating encryption-offload hardware and cloud migration to green regions. Social measures, like supply-chain transparency in the MSP agreements, tie into the SOWs. Governance pillars outline policy-management maturity, audit frequency and compliance with frameworks like FedRAMP.

FedRAMP

Federal Risk and Authorization Management Program

When we serve U.S. government clients, FedRAMP authorization becomes mandatory for cloud offerings. We map the existing GPO standards and ADCS configurations to FedRAMP's NIST

SP 800-53 control baselines, prepare System Security Plans and engage a Third-Party Assessment Organization. Post-authorization, the ISSO orchestrates continuous monitoring, checking CSP audit logs, vulnerability scans and configuration drift, submitting monthly reports to FedRAMP PMO.

HITRUST

Health Information Trust Alliance

When protecting healthcare data under HIPAA, we leverage the HITRUST CSF to harmonize multiple regulations, ISO SC 27, NIST and HIPAA, into a single framework. We shepherd the organization through a validated assessment, collecting evidence on policies (SOWs, MSA clauses), technical controls (GPOs, GCPs) and operational processes (AARs, continuous monitoring). The CSO and ISSO collaborate to remediate gaps, then engage a HITRUST-approved assessor for certification.

Knowledge Check

1. The organization plans to migrate sensitive data to a public cloud but requires a "do once, use many times" authorization to meet U.S. federal requirements. Which two frameworks guide the CSP selection and continuous monitoring?

A. SOW + MSA
B. GPO + ISSO
C. CSA STAR + FedRAMP
D. ESG + HITRUST

2. As CSO, we need executive buy-in for funding an IAM overhaul. Which metric aligns best with ESG reporting to secure both security and sustainability budgets?

A. Number of GPOs implemented
B. Count of SOW changes per quarter
C. Number of CSA STAR assessments completed
D. Reduction in data-center energy usage per CSP region

3. A healthcare provider must demonstrate unified compliance with HIPAA, NIST and ISO SC 27. Which certification framework accomplishes this and who typically oversees its governance?

A. FedRAMP, managed by the CTO
B. CSA STAR, managed by the MSP
C. ESG, managed by the NOC
D. HITRUST, managed by the ISSO

4. During contract negotiations, we need to enforce security requirements, such as vulnerability scanning and audit rights, across multiple vendors. Which two documents include those clauses?

A. CSP + CSO
B. GPO + ESG
C. MSA + SOW
D. KPI + KRI

5. The Active Directory group policies (GPOs) enforce encryption and MFA across workstations. Which role ensures those policies reflect the CSO's strategic directives and ISO SC 27 controls?

A. CTO
B. ISSO
C. MSP
D. CSA STAR assessor

6. We decide only to partner with cloud service providers that publish continuous-monitoring attestation to the CSA STAR registry. Which acronym combination validates both cloud control maturity and ongoing oversight?

A. CSP + CSA STAR
B. CSO + CTO
C. MOU + ROI
D. SLE + SLA

7. When the FedRAMP-authorized CSP changes its underlying encryption algorithm, which governance role reviews and approves that change to maintain compliance?

A. MSP
B. NOC analyst
C. ISSO
D. SRE

8. We must align the security roadmap with the company's overall technology strategy to ensure both innovation and compliance. Which two executive roles collaborate on this alignment?

A. CSO + CTO
B. CSP + ESG
C. SOW + MSA
D. GPO + PAM

9. A memorandum of understanding (MOU) with a partner mandate shared responsibility for incident response but lacks specifics on deliverables. Which document should we update to define precise security tasks and timelines?

A. GPO
B. ROI analysis
C. ESG report

D. SOW

10. The board requests proof that all high-impact systems follow healthcare-industry best practices. Which framework and evidence source provide the most direct validation?

A. FedRAMP authorization + CSP's SLA
B. HITRUST certification + assessor's report
C. CSA STAR Level 1 + MOU
D. ESG score + CSO presentation

Answer Key:

1. C

2. D

3. D

4. C

5. B

6. A

7. C

8. A

9. D

10. B

Vendor & Third-Party Management

The security program heavily depends on external partners, from cloud platforms to managed-service firms, yet each relationship introduces risk. In this section, we will explore the concepts/terminologies that vet vendors through formal processes like RFPs and NDAs, assess their security postures via SOC 3 reports, and manage risks continuously with Third-Party Risk Management (TPRM) frameworks. Then, we know that data-handling obligations fall to the Data Protection Officer (DPO) who basically ensures vendors comply with privacy regulations. And, also the remediation plans, tracked in a POAM, that drive corrective actions for identified gaps. All this will show us to weave these elements into the governance fabric. And, turn the vendor relationships into sources of resilience rather than hidden liabilities.

CSP

Cloud Service Provider

While working with a CSP does give you scalability, you're still responsible for configuration and data security. We give them detailed RFPs that ask CSPs to show they're following the rules with SOC 3 reports and FedRAMP attestations. The DPO has a look over the privacy policies and data-processing agreements before signing an NDA that restricts data use. Once the selection process is done, TPRM processes like quarterly control reviews and POAM tracking make sure the CSP deals with any problems that are found.

DPO

Data Protection Officer

The DPO is basically the privacy law expert and data-handling best practice guru for every vendor interaction. Before getting a third party involved, the DPO will check data-flow maps to make sure only the personal data needed is sent outside the systems. They negotiate contractual clauses in NDAs and MSAs that require vendors to implement appropriate safeguards, breach-notification procedures and data-subject rights support. During the yearly audits, the DPO looks over vendor compliance artefacts, SOC reports and summary of penetration tests, and signs off on any leftover risk.

NDA

Non-Disclosure Agreement

Sensitive information shared during vendor evaluations and integration is protected by requiring NDAs before any data exchange. The standard NDA template covers things like intellectual property, security architectures and customer data, and it says what the permitted uses are, how long things should be kept for and when they have to be destroyed. If we're both sharing proprietary insights or source code, we make sure we've got a mutual NDA in place. When responding to RFPs, NDAs grant access to the network diagrams and risk assessments.

POAM

Plan of Action and Milestones

After we've checked out a vendor's security controls, we log each gap we find into a POAM. This means we can then assign clear tasks to fix the issues, set due dates and specify who's responsible for each one. The regular TPRM reviews keep track of progress against these milestones and send alerts when deadlines slip or new issues come up. For example, if a CSP's penetration test reveals misconfigured firewalls, the POAM entry outlines steps to correct rules, with the CSP liaison responsible and a follow-up audit scheduled. If you see the POAM as both a work-back schedule and a progress dashboard, you can make sure that every vendor risk moves from "identified" to "resolved" without falling through the cracks.

RFP

Request for Proposal

When we're looking for new vendor partnerships, we put together an RFP that lists security requirements, compliance standards, incident-response SLAs and data-encryption expectations, as well as functional criteria. We give the RFP to the CSPs or MSSPs on our shortlist, and then we look at how they respond, using a scoring model that focuses on security. There are live Q&A sessions that explain how each vendor meets controls like vulnerability management or audit logging. Once we've scored, we'll move the top performers on to SOC 3 report reviews and reference checks. So, treat the RFP like the selection blueprint. That way, you can compare partners and choose the ones that are right for the security programme.

SOC 3

System and Organization Controls Type 3

We use SOC 3 reports to check how well vendors are controlling things without showing all the audit details. These public summaries show that third parties follow well-known rules, like Trust Services Criteria for security and availability, and get certified by independent auditors. When we review a CSP's SOC 3 report, we look for relevant control domains, note any exceptions and compare report periods against the vendor review schedule. SOC becomes a key part of the TPRM process, reducing the need for custom audits while giving us confidence that the vendors maintain controlled environments.

TPRM

Third-Party Risk Management

The TPRM programme handles the full vendor risk lifecycle: from onboarding through to offboarding when relationships end. We've got a centralised vendor registry with risk ratings based on how critical they are and how mature their control systems are. Every year or so, when there's a big contract change, automated workflows kick in and start the reassessment process. When it's integrated with the GRC platform, vendor risks end up on the same dashboards as internal control gaps.

Knowledge Check

1. You're evaluating a new cloud partner and want independent assurance of their security controls without requesting full audit details. Which document do we request?

A. NDA

B. SOC 3 report

C. POAM

D. RFP

2. Before sharing the proprietary network diagrams with a vendor for an RFP, which agreement must we have in place?
   A. CSP contract
   B. NDA
   C. SOC 3 certification
   D. POAM

3. After a gap analysis shows the CSP hasn't implemented certain encryption controls, we log actions and track deadlines. Which artifact do we use?
   A. RFP
   B. TPRM dashboard
   C. POAM
   D. NDA

4. The team issues an RFP to several MSSPs. Which section should define the minimum incident-response SLAs and data-retention requirements?
   A. POAM entries
   B. RFP security requirements
   C. SOC 3 summary
   D. NDA terms

5. As the DPO, we must ensure that third parties handle personal data in compliance with GDPR. Which role explicitly owns this responsibility?
   A. CSP account manager
   B. Data Protection Officer
   C. ISSO
   D. CSO

6. During TPRM reviews, we notice a vendor's SOC 3 report is expired. What is the immediate next step?
   A. Update the POAM with remediation tasks to obtain a current report
   B. Execute the NDA termination clause
   C. Issue a new RFP
   D. Elevate to the CSO for revocation of credentials

7. The organization's TPRM policy requires reassessment of high-criticality vendors every six months. Which process covers this lifecycle?
   A. RFP issuance
   B. NDA negotiation
   C. Continuous TPRM reviews

D. DPO certification

8. A partner misses a POAM milestone for patching their exposed API. Which two roles coordinate to enforce the next steps?
    A. CSP support engineer and RFP committee
    B. DPO and ISSO
    C. CSO and CTO
    D. NOC analyst and SOC 3 auditor

9. We need to compare vendor pricing, security posture, and support SLAs side by side before selecting a CSP. Which document do we prepare and distribute?
    A. POAM
    B. RFP
    C. NDA
    D. TPRM report

10. When offboarding a third-party service, we must ensure they no longer retain the data and revoke their access. Which governance framework step does this complete?
    A. RFP closure
    B. NDA execution
    C. TPRM offboarding
    D. SOC 3 refresh

Answer Key:

1. B
2. B
3. C
4. B
5. B
6. A
7. C
8. B
9. B
10. C

Audit, Assessment & Reporting

The proof is in the pudding, as they say, and auditing and assessment give us the evidence to show that the security programme works and to guide continual improvement. We'll be looking at standards and frameworks, from FIPS cryptographic requirements to PCI DSS payment-card controls, and we'll find out how auditors from the AICPA, under SSAE-18, assess the controls and issue SOC reports. There are governance tools like GPO that enforce configurations, and the Plan-Do-Check-Act (PDCA) cycle and risk assessments (RA) drive methodical review. And reporting metrics, like ROI on remediation investments, show stakeholders how valuable it is.

AICPA

American Institute of Certified Public Accountants

The auditors we work with are certified by the AICPA, and they help us evaluate controls over financial reporting and IT processes. Their guidance shapes SSAE-18 attestation engagements, making sure audits are consistent and trustworthy. When we get ready for a SOC audit, we use AICPA's Trust Services Criteria to make sure we've got everything covered: security, availability, processing integrity, confidentiality and privacy. We know that the audit follows professional standards, and customers and regulators worldwide accept the reports. The AICPA is basically the stamp of approval for accounting and auditing that's on every SOC report the organisation puts out.

FIPS

Federal Information Processing Standards

For government or regulated-industry systems, we always use FIPS-approved cryptographic modules. Take FIPS 140-2 validation, for instance. This certifies that an encryption library meets strict requirements for algorithm strength, key management and physical security. When we're setting up TLS on web servers, we stick to just FIPS-validated cipher suites and modules, making sure we're in line with federal rules. The GPO handles pushing those settings across Windows servers automatically. Basically, treat FIPS as the federal-grade checklist for cryptography. If we can meet its requirements, it proves that we've locked down every encryption component according to the highest standards.

GPO

Group Policy Object

When auditors check configuration baselines, they often sample GPO-enforced settings on domain-joined machines. We use GPOs to lock down registry values, disable insecure protocols and enforce patching policies in line with PCI DSS and FIPS requirements. The compliance scanning tools will flag any deviations for us to deal with. When we're doing PDCA review meetings, we tweak the GPOs to include new audit findings and then roll out new stuff to fill the gaps in our control.

PCI DSS

Payment Card Industry Data Security Standard

This is the Payment Card Industry Data Security Standard. We make sure we're PCI DSS compliant whenever we're storing, processing or transmitting cardholder data. The RA identifies scope, card-data environments versus out-of-scope segments, and the GPOs enforce controls such as network segmentation, firewalls, multi-factor authentication and encryption of data at rest. The PDCA cycle uses regular vulnerability scans and penetration tests, while SSAE-18 auditors review evidence for controls like logging and access reviews. There are reporting dashboards that track metrics like scan-remediation timelines and user-access certification completion, to show ongoing compliance.

PDCA

Plan-Do-Check-Act

We use the PDCA cycle to make improvements to any control or process. In the Plan phase, the audit-ready RA defines objectives, such as achieving SOC 2 compliance. The Do phase gets GPO-driven configurations and vendor-contracts updates up and running. When we're doing our checks, we collect evidence, vulnerability scan reports, PCI DSS self-assessments and SOC 3 summaries, and then we look at the findings to see if they match what was expected. Finally, Act is all about updating policies, adjusting control scopes or investing in training based on audit results. If you see PDCA as the way to keep making things better, each audit becomes a chance to make security controls stronger and more efficient next time.

RA

Risk Assessment

We start each audit cycle with an RA who identifies assets, threat scenarios and control gaps. We use a mix of qualitative and quantitative methods to score risks, like potential PCI DSS fines or breach-remediation costs, to figure out what to work on first. The results of the RA feed into both PDCA planning and audit scope definition, so they guide which controls auditors will test. When we present RA findings to the CSO and board, we include ROI estimates for proposed control investments.

ROI

Return on Investment

When you're planning the budget for projects that are driven by audits, whether that's FIPS-validated HSMs or PCI DSS-compliant network segmentation, it's really important to have clear ROI calculations. We estimate cost savings from avoided fines, faster incident responses and better operational efficiency, then compare those benefits to project costs. If you include ROI in the audit report summary, it'll help to show why funding is needed for control improvements. The people involved like it when we link compliance investments to real business results, not just ticking boxes.

SSAE-18

Statement on Standards for Attestation Engagements No. 18

When we're audited by a service organisation, SSAE-18 tells us what standards the auditor has to follow. We put together a System Description, explaining the governance, risk and control environment, and we back this up with evidence like GPO snapshots and RA documentation. The auditor tests controls over a reporting period, then issues a SOC report based on the Trust Services Criteria. The SSAE-18's focus on complementary user controls makes sure customers know which responsibilities are theirs. Just remember to use SSAE-18 as the procedural rulebook for every SOC engagement, and you'll get consistent and reliable audit outcomes.

SOC

System and Organization Controls

Reports from the SOC, whether Type '1 or Type '2, independently validate the control environment. The first one looks at financial reporting controls, while the second and third ones check security, availability, processing integrity, confidentiality and privacy. We pick the right report for what the stakeholders need. SOC 3 gives a general overview for the public, while SOC 2 gives the detailed results of the auditor tests. The GPO and RA artefacts are at the heart of the SOC evidence package, and PDCA iterations drive continuous control improvements between audit periods.

Knowledge Check

1. When selecting a cryptographic library for a federal-government system, which standard must we enforce and validate?

A. PCI DSS
B. FIPS
C. SOC 3
D. PDCA

2. During an audit, the SOC 2 Type 2 report us follows attestation guidelines set by which standard-setting body?

A. AICPA
B. PCI DSS
C. GPO
D. RA

3. Automating registry lockdowns and password policies across Windows servers to meet audit baselines uses which enforcement mechanism?
   A. SSAE-18
   B. GPO
   C. ROI
   D. PDCA

4. The PCI DSS RA indicates that cardholder-data environments must be segregated from other networks. Which two control definitions enforce this?
   A. FIPS and SOC 3
   B. GPO and PCI DSS network controls
   C. AICPA and PDCA
   D. SSAE-18 and ROI

5. We apply the Plan-Do-Check-Act cycle to remediate audit findings. Which phase involves collecting vulnerability-scan results and control test evidence?
   A. Plan
   B. Do
   C. Check
   D. Act

6. Calculating the cost-benefit of deploying a FIPS-validated HSM versus potential breach recovery costs uses which metric?
   A. SOC
   B. ROI
   C. PDCA
   D. RA

7. When preparing for a SOC 3 report, we gather control-operation evidence for at least six months, as required by which attestation standard?
   A. SSAE-18
   B. PCI DSS
   C. FIPS
   D. AICPA

8. An auditor spots that the server configurations deviate from the documented baseline

GPOs. Which aspect of the audit-readiness needs improvement?

A. PDCA maintenance of GPOs
B. ROI calculation accuracy
C. CSP selection process
D. SOC report type

9. Which framework harmonizes multiple regulations into a single self-assessment for cloud-security best practices, simplifying PCI DSS and SSAE-18 mappings?

A. PDCA
B. CSA STAR
C. FIPS
D. MOU

10. After Act phase improvements, we schedule the next audit as part of which continuous cycle?

A. RA only
B. PDCA
C. ROI updates
D. D. NDA renewal

Answer Key:

1. B
2. A
3. B
4. B
5. C
6. B
7. A
8. A
9. B
10. B

Training, Awareness & Metrics

You can't build a security-savvy culture just by issuing policies. You also need to engage, educate, measure progress and keep refining your approach. That means our training programmes will earn CPE credits, we'll deliver interactive courses via the LMS and apply the PDCA cycle to improve every session. And measuring learning outcomes and linking them to business value with ROI calculations turns abstract awareness efforts into tangible insights.

CPE

Continuing Professional Education

The security training is set up so that team members can qualify for CPE credits, so everyone can keep their certifications up to date. This includes CISSPs who need 120 CPEs every three years, and auditors who are working towards AICPA requirements. Every course is set up to include learning objectives, attendance tracking and post-training assessments to meet the standards of the CPE audit. The LMS automatically issues certificates with CPE-hour summaries, and then reports completions to the certification bodies. If you link the curriculum to formal credit systems, learners will stay on track and the programme will meet industry standards.

LMS

Learning Management System

When Phishing Awareness, secure coding or data-privacy obligations are launched, they're published on the LMS. It's all about setting up learning paths, enrolling groups based on their roles, and setting deadlines for completing mandatory CPE components. It's got built-in analytics that show progress rates, quiz scores and where learners are dropping out of modules, so we can see where they're struggling. There are automated reminders to nudge users who fall behind, and gamification elements like badges and leaderboards to boost engagement.

ROI

Return on Investment

If you can show the boss how the training is going to make money, they'll be more likely to keep it going and even make it bigger. There are a few ways they can save money, like by reducing how long it takes to respond to incidents, spending less on phishing remediation, and getting better results from audits compared to the costs of development and delivery. So, say there's a 70% drop in successful phishing attacks after awareness training, saving 200 staff hours a quarter. That's like a win for us, but we've also got to think about the LMS licensing and facilitator fees. If you show the return on investment in clear dollar terms, you can link educational activities to business performance. That makes the security-training programme an investment rather than a line-item expense.

Knowledge Check

1. The team needs to earn credits to maintain their CISSP certifications. Which metric tracks those required educational hours?

A. ROI
B. CPE
C. PDCA
D. LMS

2. Rolling out a new phishing-awareness course, we enroll all users, set completion deadlines and monitor progress. Which system are we using?
   A. LMS
   B. ROI
   C. CPE
   D. PDCA

3. After delivering a workshop, we analyze quiz pass-rates and feedback surveys before redesigning the content. Which step of the PDCA cycle is this?
   A. Plan
   B. Do
   C. Check
   D. Act

4. We compare the cost of building an interactive security lab against the dollars saved by reduced incident-response time. Which calculation are we performing?
   A. CPE
   B. PDCA
   C. ROI
   D. LMS

5. Ensuring each employee completes 20 hours of approved training per year supports compliance with which requirement?
   A. ROI
   B. PDCA
   C. CPE
   D. LMS

6. Noticing that only 40 % of participants finish an online module, we shorten videos and add quizzes. Which PDCA phase does this represent?
   A. Plan
   B. Do
   C. Check
   D. Act

7. A dashboard shows 95 % course completion but indicates most scores cluster around 60 %. Which PDCA phase involves interpreting those results?
    A. Do
    B. Check
    C. Act
    D. Plan

8. Presenting to executives, we demonstrate that each training dollar yields five dollars in avoided breach costs. Which acronym describes this measure?
    A. LMS
    B. CPE
    C. ROI
    D. PDCA

9. Issuing digital certificates that record learning hours and topics automatically ties into which system's functionality?
    A. CPE
    B. LMS
    C. ROI
    D. PDCA

10. Scheduling recurring refresher courses, updating content based on feedback and measuring improved performance completes which improvement loop?
    A. ROI
    B. LMS
    C. PDCA
    D. CPE

Answer Key:

1. B
2. A
3. C
4. C
5. C
6. D
7. B
8. C
9. B

10. C

PRACTICE EXAM

Part I: General Security Concepts (18 Questions)

1. Which model breaks each authentication transaction into three phases, verification, policy check and audit logging?
   A. 2FA
   B. AAA
   C. MFA
   D. IAMaaS

2. A network administrator implements an Access Control List on a router to block traffic from specific IP addresses. Which acronym describes this control?
   A. ACL
   B. AUP
   C. API
   D. AP

3. Employees agree not to install personal file-sharing software on workstations under which policy?
   A. ACL
   B. AUP
   C. CSPM
   D. CASB

4. When personal devices connect to corporate resources but remain subject to company controls, this approach is called:
   A. BYOD
   B. COBO
   C. COPE
   D. CYOD

5. An organization issues devices to employees that cannot install unauthorized apps. Which acronym applies?
   A. BYOD
   B. COBO
   C. COPE

D. CSP

6. Forcing users to provide both a password and a hardware token illustrates:
A. AAA
B. 2FA
C. RBAC
D. PSK

7. Which protocol negotiates a secure tunnel before transmitting user credentials for Wi-Fi authentication?
A. PAP
B. PEAP
C. RADIUS
D. TACACS+

8. Pre-shared keys used in WPA2-Personal fall under which acronym?
A. PAP
B. PSK
C. AES
D. P12

9. A centralized server that handles authentication, authorization and accounting for network devices is typically:
A. RADIUS
B. ACL
C. CYOD
D. CSPM

10. Assigning permissions based on job functions rather than individuals defines:
A. RBAC
B. PDP
C. PAM
D. PDCA

11. Which cloud control tool continuously monitors configurations against policy frameworks?
A. CSPM
B. CSP
C. CPA
D. CSV

12. DNS over HTTPS and DNS over TLS are referenced by which acronyms?
  A. DoH and DoT
  B. DHE and DLL
  C. DNSSEC and ESP
  D. EDR and EFS

13. A phishing-resistant authentication standard that uses public-key cryptography is:
  A. FIDO2
  B. MFA
  C. TACACS+
  D. SPIM

14. When we outsource IAM to a cloud provider via API calls, we are using:
  A. IAMaaS
  B. PaaS
  C. SaaS
  D. CSPM

15. Standardizing identity data exchange using SCIM ensures interoperability between:
  A. SOAP services
  B. OID and OU
  C. SaaS applications
  D. SIEM systems

16. Machine identities in service-to-service authentication within Kubernetes clusters often leverage:
  A. SPIFFE
  B. CSP
  C. PAP
  D. SOC

17. Which orchestrator issues short-lived certificates to workloads using SPIRE?
  A. SPIFFE
  B. FIPS
  C. SCCM
  D. SOC

18. Implementing least-privilege network access based on identity tags leverages:

A. IAMaaS
B. SDAutomation
C. SD-WAN
D. SASE

Part II: Threats, Vulnerabilities & Mitigations (18 Questions)

19. A prolonged, stealthy campaign that harvests data from the network over months is known as:
A. XSS
B. APT
C. DoS
D. ESN

20. Thousands of bots flooding the site with requests describe which attack?
A. DoS
B. ROP
C. DDoS
D. RFI

21. An exploit technique that repurposes existing code snippets is:
A. RAT
B. ROP
C. RCE
D. OVAL

22. Identifying password-reset CSRF vulnerabilities in a web form address:
A. XSRF
B. LFI
C. SQLi
D. PUP

23. Which threat-actor intelligence framework provides a taxonomy of attacker behaviors?
A. ATT&CK
B. CVSS
C. NVD

D. CSI

24. Annualized Loss Expectancy (ALE) is calculated by multiplying Single Loss Expectancy (SLE) by:
A. ARO
B. ROI
C. KPI
D. RTO

25. On-device malware detection and prevention are core functions of:
A. AV
B. RAT
C. RDP
D. DLP

26. An exploit that includes malicious VBA macros in Office documents leverages:
A. BASH
B. VBA
C. SQLi
D. PAP

27. Attacks that trick email recipients with spoofed executive messages fall under:
A. BEC
B. CSRF
C. CHAP
D. FDE

28. Identifying indicator hashes and domains for threat hunting uses:
A. IOC
B. IOU
C. IBS
D. ICE

29. When we share and consume threat intelligence events, we likely use:
A. SSI
B. MISP
C. SOAP
D. SAML

30. Automated workflows that orchestrate detection and response across tools describe:
A. SOAR
B. SIP
C. SOAP
D. SNS

31. The National Vulnerability Database maps CVEs to:
A. CWE
B. CSV
C. CRM
D. CRC

32. Automating vulnerability checks with an XML schema reference:
A. OVAL
B. ACL
C. CSPM
D. DNSSEC

33. Industrial-control-system security is governed by which standard?
A. ISO 27001
B. IEC 62443
C. PCI DSS
D. SOC

34. During attack reconnaissance, harvesting user profiles from social media is:
A. ESN
B. OSINT
C. RAT
D. OSPF

35. Embedded backdoors installed via phishing attachments describe:
A. RCE
B. RAT
C. SQLi
D. CSV

36. Indicators of compromise like file hashes and malicious IPs are best described as:
A. ECU
B. IOC

C. OID
D. PIM

37. To automate prioritized patching based on criticality and ROI, we integrate vulnerability data with:
A. SOAR
B. IAMaaS
C. TIP
D. POAM

Part III: Security Architecture (18 Questions)

38. Preventing loops in Ethernet segments relies on exchanging which frames?
A. ARP
B. BPDU
C. DNS
D. ADCS

39. Encapsulating IP packets inside new headers across the Internet uses:
A. NAT
B. GRE
C. LAN
D. SAN

40. Extending the LAN to remote clients via PPP frames over IP describes:
A. L2TP
B. MPLS
C. VXLAN
D. VPC

41. Logical segmentation within a single switch port that isolates traffic is a:
A. VLAN
B. MAN
C. SDN
D. CDN

42. Overlaying millions of segments across data centers uses which technology?
A. MPLS

B. VXLAN
C. NAT
D. DNSSEC

43. Dynamic path selection across multiple WAN links describes:
A. SD-WAN
B. SDN
C. NAT
D. VPN

44. A control-plane separation architecture managed by a central controller is:
A. GPO
B. SDN
C. DNSSEC
D. SNMP

45. Translating private addresses to public while hiding internal topology uses:
A. VLAN
B. NAT
C. ACL
D. CCMP

46. A carrier-grade MPLS VPN that isolates customer traffic via labels is:
A. MPLS
B. L2TP
C. GRE
D. SD-WAN

47. Infrastructure definitions declared in code and managed via plans and applies use:
A. ARM
B. Terraform
C. Ansible
D. LDAP

48. Provisioning bare-metal servers through an API as if they were virtual uses:
A. MaaS
B. PaaS
C. SaaS
D. CSI

49. Deploying runtime environments and middleware under provider management refers to:
A. IaaS
B. PaaS
C. PKI
D. FDE

50. Fully managed application suites, email, CRM, are delivered as:
A. SaaS
B. IaaS
C. MaaS
D. VDI

51. Centralized secure desktop pools accessed over the network define:
A. VPC
B. VDI
C. CNI
D. CSI

52. An isolated cloud network with subnets, route tables and security groups is called:
A. VPC
B. VLAN
C. VPN
D. NAT

53. Predicting average uptime based on component reliability and repair rates relies on:
A. RPO
B. MTBF
C. ROI
D. IAM

54. The acceptable data-loss point in time defines:
A. RTO
B. RPO
C. MTTF
D. SLA

55. Protecting the boot sector against tampering with checksum validation is:
A. MBR

B. ACL
C. DNS
D. NTFS

56. Ensuring each disk sector is encrypted with a unique tweak uses which mode?
A. CBC
B. XTS
C. GCM
D. CRC

57. A protocol that combines counter-mode encryption with integrity tags is:
A. CFB
B. AES-256
C. GCM
D. CCMP

Part IV: Security Operations (18 Questions)

58. Collecting metrics via HTTP endpoints every minute uses which interface?
A. SNMP
B. Telemetry API
C. Syslog
D. CWPP

59. Agents that monitor file integrity and block privilege escalation in the cloud are part of a:
A. CWPP
B. CSPM
C. DLP
D. GPO

60. Aggregating logs into Elasticsearch, Logstash and Kibana defines:
A. ELK
B. SIEM
C. NIDS
D. WAF

61. Restricting user-access based on device GPS coordinates implements:
A. GPS geo-fencing

B. NAT
C. RADIUS
D. LDAP

62. The difference between service performance metrics and risk indicators is captured by:
A. KPI vs. KRI
B. SLE vs. SLA
C. RPO vs. RTO
D. ROI vs. PES

63. Synchronizing host clocks for accurate logs uses:
A. NTP
B. SNMP
C. SOC
D. LDAP

64. Polling switch port errors and CPU load every five minutes leverages:
A. SSH
B. SNMP
C. CSI
D. RMM

65. Centralized forwarding of system events from servers and appliances uses:
A. SSH
B. Syslog
C. RMM
D. SIEM

66. Firmware-level secure-boot violations are captured by:
A. UEFI
B. BIOS
C. ELK
D. KPI

67. AI-powered anomaly detection and event correlation platforms are known as:
A. SOAR
B. AIOps
C. TIP
D. CRT

68. JSON message streams that buffer and replay events use:
A. Kafka
B. Fluentd
C. REST
D. SDK

69. An agentless orchestration tool using YAML playbooks is:
A. Ansible
B. Chef
C. Puppet
D. Terraform

70. Visualization dashboards querying Prometheus metrics are built in:
A. Grafana
B. Kibana
C. Splunk
D. SIEM

71. Endpoint-level detection and response platforms are abbreviated as:
A. EDR
B. DLP
C. NIDS
D. IDS

72. Incident-response run-books and playbooks automated across tools describe:
A. SOAR
B. SOC
C. SRE
D. SSO

73. Remote execution and patch management across endpoints use:
A. RMM
B. LDAP
C. SOAP
D. JSON

74. Deep syscall capture and container-level rules are provided by:
A. Fluentd

B. Sysdig
C. CWPP
D. EDR

Part V: Program Management & Oversight (18 Questions)

75. A chief officer who aligns security strategy with business objectives holds the title:
A. CSO
B. CTO
C. CSP
D. CFO

76. The on-prem PKI role that issues and manages certificates in Active Directory is:
A. ADCS
B. ADFS
C. ISSO
D. CSPM

77. Enabling single sign-on across multiple web apps with SAML uses which role?
A. IdP
B. PAM
C. PDP
D. EDR

78. Controlling highest-privilege credentials with vault check-out and recording describes:
A. MFA
B. PAM
C. AUP
D. LDAP

79. A registry that catalogs cloud providers' self-assessments and certifications is:
A. CSA STAR
B. CSA
C. NOC
D. CSI

80. Third-Party Risk Management processes track vendor lifecycles and remediation via:
A. TPRM
B. POAM
C. NDA
D. SCP

81. An agreement that defines general legal terms for all engagements is a:
A. MSA
B. SOW
C. NDA
D. RFP

82. The control-evaluation reports issued under SSAE-18 are called:
A. SOC
B. SAML
C. SLA
D. SLE

83. Continuous-improvement cycles for both governance and operations follow:
A. PDCA
B. SLA
C. ROI
D. RTO

84. Selecting encryption modules validated against U.S. government standards relies on:
A. FIPS
B. PCI DSS
C. ROI
D. AICPA

85. Metrics showing uptime guarantees and penalties reside in:
A. SLA
B. SLE
C. MOU
D. SOC

86. Tracking training hours for certification maintenance requires:
A. CPE
B. LMS

C. ROI
D. KPI

87. A service-level metric that warns before thresholds breach performance targets is a:
A. KRI
B. KPI
C. ROI
D. SLA

88. Automated dashboards in the NOC that display Prometheus metrics use which tool?
A. Grafana
B. Kibana
C. ELK
D. SIEM

89. Defining multi-year cost savings against security investments measures:
A. ROI
B. PDCA
C. SOW
D. MSA

90. Simulated phishing, quizzes and compliance tracking in the LMS measure the success of:
A. Training & Awareness
B. TPRM
C. FedRAMP
D. SOC

Answers (with explanation)

1. (B) **AAA**
AAA stands for Authentication, Authorization, Accounting, covering verify identity, enforce policies, and log actions.

2. (A) **ACL**
Access Control List rules on routers allow or deny traffic based on IP, port, protocol.

3. (B) **AUP**

An Acceptable Use Policy specifies allowed/disallowed behaviors, such as banning personal file-sharing.

4. (A) **BYOD**
   Bring The Own Device allows employee-owned devices to access corporate resources under controls.

5. (B) **COBO**
   Company-Owned, Business-Only devices prevent installing unauthorized apps yet remain under corporate control.

6. (B) **2FA**
   Two-Factor Authentication pairs something we know with something us have (e.g., password + token).

7. (B) **PEAP**
   Protected EAP establishes a TLS tunnel before inner authentication, protecting credentials on Wi-Fi.

8. (B) **PSK**
   Pre-Shared Key is the secret used in WPA2-Personal to authenticate wireless devices.

9. (A) **RADIUS**
   Remote Authentication Dial-In User Service centralizes AAA for network access devices.

10. (A) **RBAC**
    Role-Based Access Control grants permissions by role rather than individual identity.

11. (A) **CSPM**
    Cloud Security Posture Management continuously monitors cloud configurations against policy.

12. (A) **DoH and DoT**
    DNS over HTTPS (DoH) and DNS over TLS (DoT) encrypt DNS queries to protect privacy.

13. (A) **FIDO2**

Fast IDentity Online 2 uses public-key crypto for phishing-resistant authentication (e.g., hardware keys).

14. (A) **IAMaaS**
Identity and Access Management as a Service offloads IAM functions to a cloud provider.

15. (C) **SaaS applications**
System for Cross-domain Identity Management (SCIM) standardizes user provisioning and deprovisioning across SaaS.

16. (A) **SPIFFE**
Secure Production Identity Framework For Everyone issues workload identities in cloud environments.

17. (A) **SPIFFE**
SPIFFE issues identities; SPIRE is its runtime implementation distributing SPIFFE IDs.

18. (D) **SASE**
(Not listed in choices) Actually segmentation via identity tags often leverages SASE architectures.

19. (B) **APT**
Advanced Persistent Threats are long-term, stealthy campaigns targeting specific organizations.

20. (C) **DDoS**
Distributed Denial of Service floods targets with traffic from multiple sources.

21. (B) **ROP**
Return-Oriented Programming chains small code snippets to bypass memory protections.

22. (A) **XSRF**
Cross-Site Request Forgery (CSRF/XSRF) tricks browsers into submitting unauthorized requests.

23. (A) **ATT&CK**
MITRE ATT&CK provides a matrix of adversary tactics, techniques, and procedures.

24. (A) **ARO**
Annualized Rate of Occurrence (ARO) multiplies with SLE to yield ALE.

25. (A) **AV**
Anti-Virus software detects and blocks known malware signatures on hosts.

26. (B) **VBA**
Visual Basic for Applications macros can be weaponized to deliver malware from documents.

27. (A) **BEC**
Business Email Compromise uses spear-phishing to impersonate executives for fraud.

28. (A) **IOC**
Indicators of Compromise include file hashes, IPs or domains known to be malicious.

29. (B) **MISP**
Malware Information Sharing Platform enables collaborative threat-intelligence exchange.

30. (A) **SOAR**
Security Orchestration, Automation and Response automates workflows across security tools.

31. (A) **CWE**
Common Weakness Enumeration categorizes types of software flaws underlying CVEs.

32. (A) **OVAL**
Open Vulnerability and Assessment Language standardizes automated checks for security configurations.

33. (B) **IEC 62443**
Industrial Control Systems (ICS) security standard for manufacturing and critical infrastructure.

34. (B) **OSINT**
Open-Source Intelligence refers to collecting information from public sources.

35. (B) **RAT**
Remote Access Trojans provide persistent, covert control over compromised machines.

36. (B) **IOC**
Indicators of Compromise alert defenders to known malicious artifacts in their environment.

37. (C) **TIP**
Threat Intelligence Platforms integrate and prioritize vulnerability and threat data to guide patching.

38. (B) **BPDU**
Bridge Protocol Data Units coordinate Spanning Tree Protocol to prevent loops.

39. (B) **GRE**
Generic Routing Encapsulation creates point-to-point tunnels by encapsulating IP packets.

40. (A) **L2TP**
Layer 2 Tunneling Protocol extends Ethernet segments by tunneling PPP frames over IP.

41. (A) **VLAN**
Virtual LAN segments traffic logically within a shared switch or network.

42. (B) **VXLAN**
Virtual Extensible LAN encapsulates Ethernet in UDP, supporting millions of logical segments.

43. (A) **SD-WAN**
Software-Defined WAN dynamically routes traffic over multiple links based on performance.

44. (B) **SDN**
Software-Defined Networking separates control and data planes, enabling centralized management.

45. (B) **NAT**

Network Address Translation hides private addresses and conserves IPv4 space.

46. (A) **MPLS**
Multiprotocol Label Switching uses labels for traffic engineering and VPN segmentation.

47. (B) **Terraform**
Terraform uses declarative HCL to define infrastructure across providers and manage state.

48. (A) **MaaS**
Metal as a Service provisions bare-metal servers via API like virtual machines.

49. (B) **PaaS**
Platform as a Service provides managed runtime environments and scaling.

50. (A) **SaaS**
Software as a Service delivers fully managed applications like email or CRM.

51. (B) **VDI**
Virtual Desktop Infrastructure hosts desktop sessions centrally and delivers them over the network.

52. (A) **VPC**
Virtual Private Cloud isolates cloud workloads in defined subnets and security groups.

53. (B) **MTBF**
Mean Time Between Failures estimates average interval between hardware failures.

54. (B) **RPO**
Recovery Point Objective defines acceptable data-loss window before an outage.

55. (A) **MBR**
Master Boot Record is the first sector on disk; protecting it prevents boot-sector malware.

56. (B) **XTS**
XTS-AES uses tweaks per disk sector to ensure each encryption block is unique.

57. (C) **GCM**
Galois/Counter Mode combines counter-mode encryption with authentication tags.

58. (B) **Telemetry API**
APIs expose metrics endpoints (e.g., Prometheus) for scraping system and application data.

59. (A) **CWPP**
Cloud Workload Protection Platforms deploy agents to monitor and enforce runtime security in clouds.

60. (A) **ELK**
Elasticsearch, Logstash, and Kibana centralize, parse and visualize logs at scale.

61. (A) **GPS geo-fencing**
Using device GPS coordinates to enforce location-based access rules.

62. (A) **KPI vs. KRI**
KPIs measure performance, KRIs warn of risks before they impact KPIs.

63. (A) **NTP**
Network Time Protocol synchronizes clocks for consistent timestamps across systems.

64. (B) **SNMP**
Simple Network Management Protocol polls network devices for health metrics like interface errors.

65. (B) **Syslog**
Standard protocol for forwarding system and application logs to central collectors.

66. (A) **UEFI**
Unified Extensible Firmware Interface secure-boot logs hardware integrity checks at boot.

67. (B) **AIOps**
Artificial Intelligence for IT Operations applies ML to large telemetry streams for anomaly detection.

68. (A) **Kafka**

Distributed streaming platform for high-throughput, durable publish/subscribe event delivery.

69. (A) **Ansible**
Agentless orchestration tool using YAML playbooks to automate configuration and remediation.

70. (A) **Grafana**
Visualization and alerting front-end for time-series databases like Prometheus.

71. (A) **EDR**
Endpoint Detection and Response platforms provide deep telemetry and automated containment.

72. (A) **SOAR**
Security Orchestration, Automation and Response integrates tools and automates playbooks.

73. (A) **RMM**
Remote Monitoring and Management platforms centrally control patching, scripting and configuration across endpoints.

74. (B) **Sysdig**
Container- and cloud-native observability platform capturing syscalls and metrics for security and performance.

75. (A) **CSO**
Chief Security Officer leads security strategy and governance at the executive level.

76. (A) **ADCS**
Active Directory Certificate Services provides on-prem PKI functionality within Windows domains.

77. (A) **IdP**
Identity Provider issues authentication tokens (SAML/OIDC) enabling Single Sign-On.

78. (B) **PAM**

Privileged Access Management vaults and records the use of high-privilege credentials.

79. (A) **CSA STAR**
Cloud Security Alliance's Security, Trust & Assurance Registry catalogs cloud provider assessments.

80. (A) **TPRM**
Third-Party Risk Management encompasses vendor onboarding, monitoring and offboarding processes.

81. (A) **MSA**
Master Service Agreement sets broad contractual terms for all engagements with a vendor.

82. (A) **SOC**
System and Organization Controls reports evaluate service-organization controls under SSAE-18.

83. (A) **PDCA**
Plan-Do-Check-Act is the continuous-improvement cycle applied to governance and operations.

84. (A) **FIPS**
Federal Information Processing Standards validate cryptographic modules for U.S. government use.

85. (A) **SLA**
Service-Level Agreement specifies uptime, performance guarantees and associated remedies.

86. (A) **CPE**
Continuing Professional Education credits are tracked to maintain certifications.

87. (A) **KRI**
Key Risk Indicators alert on conditions that threaten performance before KPIs degrade.

88. (A) **Grafana**
Dashboards for Prometheus metrics are typically built in Grafana.

89. (A) **ROI**
Return on Investment measures financial benefit of security and reliability projects.

90. (A) **Training & Awareness**
LMS-delivered phishing drills, quizzes and tracking support the Training & Awareness program.

Index

E

F

G

H

I

J

K

L

M

N

O

P

Q

R

S

T

U

V

W

X

Y

Epilogue

In my professional opinion, obtaining certification should be regarded as a starting point rather than an end goal. The ability to pass Security Plus demonstrates an understanding of how to map controls to outcomes. The subsequent steps depend on the path we want to take. If operations and detection are of interest to you, I would recommend pursuing CompTIA CySA Plus to enhance SIEM and threat-hunting skills, followed by a cloud security specialisation to master detection across hybrid environments. If we are interested in offensive work, PenTest plus will provide us with practical test techniques, and the Offensive Security Certified Professional will teach us adversary tradecraft at a deeper, hands-on level. For those interested in pursuing a career in program management or leadership roles, holding a Certified Information Systems Security Professional (CISSP) or Certified Information Systems Manager (CISM) certification can be advantageous. Certifications like these provide a solid foundation in enterprise controls, policy, and risk management.

I would recommend combining formal qualifications with practical projects, ensuring that each certificate demonstrates specific skills and expertise. In order to defend the architectures we expect, it is advisable to build a home lab that mirrors them. In preparation for interviews, please convert three exam concepts into small projects that we can present. These could include an automated SIEM alert pipeline, a hardened SSH bastion with PAM integration, or a scripted containment and evidence collection playbook. There are two ways we can get involved. We can either join a Capture the Flag team or contribute to an open source security tool. Such artefacts carry more weight than a simple list of letters on a CV.

It is also advisable to maintain a consistent practice schedule. It is also responsible for scheduling weekly lab sessions, monthly mock incidents and quarterly reviews of new standards and protocols. A pair study should be conducted in conjunction with one measurable outcome that can be tracked. Some examples of such outcomes include reduced MTTR, improved detection coverage or closed POA&Ms. We kindly ask us to keep a concise portfolio describing the problem, the implementation and the result. Such evidence can help us translate certification into career momentum.

There is a growing body of evidence to suggest that community can accelerate growth. In order to develop professionally, it is advisable to find a mentor, attend local chapter meetings and participate in online forums where practitioners share their experiences and knowledge. We recommend that we teach what we have learnt, as mentoring consolidates knowledge faster than solo study. It is imperative that a tight set of goals is established for the next 12 months, with any necessary adjustments to be made as opportunities arise.

Those who follow a project-driven path and a targeted certification plan will transition from certification to sustained contribution within any security team.

Thank You

www.ingramcontent.com/pod-product-compliance
Lightning Source LLC
Chambersburg PA
CBHW080213170726
48282CB00030B/1100
* 9 7 8 9 3 4 9 1 7 4 9 7 9 *